The Cyclist's Mind

Jamie Borg

Copyright © 2024 Jamie Borg

All rights reserved.

ISBN: 978-1-0683310-3-9

DEDICATION

Without the support of my family, especially my amazing wife Ria, our brood Felix, Farrah and Chester and my parents. I wouldn't be able to do what I do, so this is for you all, with all my love.

This is also dedicated to all the people all over the world who take pleasure at the sheer joy of riding bikes , wave and say hello no matter how tired their legs are, and make cycling the community that it is.

CONTENTS

	Preface	i
1	Introduction: Unlocking the Cyclist's Mind	Pg 1
2	The History of Self-Hypnosis	Pg 13
3	The Science of Self Hypnosis	Pg 21
4	Real Life Case Studies	Pg 33
5	'Doing' Self Hypnosis: Overview	Pg 39
6	'Doing' Self Hypnosis: Inductions	Pg 49
7	The Power of Language	Pg 61
8	Visualization	Pg 73
9	Pain Management	Pg 87
10	'The Robot'	Pg 95
11	From Relaxed to Alert	Pg 101
12	Altered States & Flow	Pg 111
13	Mental Toughness	Pg 125
14	Setbacks & 'Failures'	Pg 135

THE CYCLIST'S MIND

15	Recovery	Pg 143
16	Troubleshooting Your Self Hypnosis	Pg 153
17	Seasonal Strategies	Pg 161
18	Mental Tools for Group Ride & Team Dynamics	Pg 169

PREFACE

The human mind has always fascinated me. As an ICU nurse, I spent countless hours at the bedside, witnessing firsthand the incredible resilience—and fragility—of the human body and spirit.

It was during those years in the ICU that my curiosity about the power of the mind took root. I became intrigued by the ways we could harness it to influence not just our thoughts, but our physiology, performance, and overall well-being. That curiosity eventually led me to hypnosis—a practice that seemed to bridge the gap between science and the extraordinary.

I'll admit, at first, I was sceptical. Like many, my understanding of hypnosis was shaped by clichés and misconceptions. But as I delved into the research and explored the techniques myself, I realized that hypnosis wasn't about surrendering control or entering some mysterious trance. It was about accessing the deeper parts of the mind—the subconscious—and learning to influence it for positive change.

As I studied more, I couldn't help but wonder: if hypnosis could reduce pain, aid recovery, and even help manage chronic conditions, what else could it do? What if this tool, often reserved for therapeutic settings, could be used by anyone—cyclists, athletes, or anyone seeking an edge—to enhance focus, resilience, and performance?

Cycling has always been a passion of mine, and as although I trained initially as a Clinical Hypnotherapist, I began to integrate self-hypnosis techniques into my own rides, the results were transformative. I found myself pushing through mental and physical barriers with newfound clarity and ease. Pain became manageable, focus sharpened, and moments of self-doubt quieted. It wasn't long before I realized that this powerful tool could benefit countless others, especially in a sport where the mind plays such a pivotal role and began to work with cyclists through my practice Hypno Velo (www.hypnovelo.com).

This book is the culmination of my journey—from an ICU nurse captivated by the mind's potential to a devoted advocate for the power of self-hypnosis and Sports Hypnotherapist. My goal is simple: to show you how to tap into the remarkable capabilities of your own mind, to not only improve your performance on the bike but to enhance your mental resilience, focus, and confidence in all areas of life.

Self-hypnosis is not a magical fix; it's a skill—a learnable, practical tool that you can adapt to your needs. Whether you want to manage pain, reduce nerves, unlock flow states, or push past personal limits, self-hypnosis offers a pathway to greater control over your thoughts and emotions.

The techniques that are contained in this book aren't just able to transform your cycling, when you apply the knowledge into your wider, everyday life you will see that it can also transform how you parent and work.

I wrote this book to demystify hypnosis and to make it accessible to anyone willing to explore its potential. You don't need to be a professional cyclist or a mental health expert to benefit. You simply need a willingness to learn, practice, and apply these techniques.

Is this a complete guide to hypnosis which teaches you every single technique possible? Have concepts such as consciousness and subconsciousness explained all current cognitive neuroscience theories about them? Absolutely not. I am certain that some will raise as criticism that I haven't taught you 'hypnotic phenomena' (techniques where thinks like arms lifting into the air by imaging balloons attached to them for example) has been completely omitted. My aim for this book is to give you the cyclist a practical roadmap and guide of what self-hypnosis is and ultimately, how to use it as a tool to help you both on and off the bike and that is precisely why I have selected the specific, proven techniques and tools you'll find in this book.

As you turn these pages, I invite you to set aside any preconceived notions you may have about hypnosis and approach this with an open mind. Whether you're preparing for a big race, tackling tough climbs, or simply striving to be a more resilient and focused version of yourself, the tools in this book can guide you toward breakthroughs you never thought possible.

The mind is a powerful ally. It's my hope that this book will inspire you to harness its potential, just as it inspired me all those years ago in the ICU. Together, let's explore how the art and science of self-hypnosis can elevate your cycling—and your life.

– Jamie Borg

1 UNLOCKING THE CYCLISTS MIND

Cycling is a sport with many personalities. A lot of the time it's one the most pleasurable things you can do. The very simple joy of just moving on two wheels really cannot be overstated, riding a bike can really become a transcending experience. But anyone who's spent time in the saddle knows it's far more complex. Beyond the physical effort, cycling demands mental strength, emotional resilience, and an ability to focus for long stretches. Whether you're climbing a relentless hill, chasing the pack in a race, or grinding through a solo ride, your mental game can be the difference between pushing through or giving up.

This book is about helping you win that mental battle. By mastering self-hypnosis, you'll gain tools to train your mind, overcome challenges, and unlock a new level of performance on the bike. From calming pre-race nerves to managing pain and discomfort, self-hypnosis is a proven method that has helped countless athletes achieve their goals—and it can help you too.

Mental Challenges Cyclists Face

To fully understand the value of self-hypnosis, it helps to take a closer look at the unique mental challenges cyclists face. These obstacles, while daunting, are also opportunities for growth when approached with the right mindset and tools.

The Loneliness of the Long Ride

Cycling can be an isolating sport, especially during long solo rides. Without external distractions, your mind is left to wander, often focusing on doubts, fatigue, or discomfort. The ability to quiet negative thoughts and stay mentally engaged during these stretches is crucial to making the ride not only bearable but enjoyable.

Managing Pain and Discomfort

Cyclists are no strangers to pain or discomfort—whether it's the burning in your quads during a climb or the ache of being in the saddle for hours. Pain can dominate your thoughts and make you want to quit, but reframing discomfort as a sign of progress can help you push through tough moments.

Performance Anxiety

The pressure to perform can be overwhelming, especially before races or big events. The fear of failure or the weight of expectations often triggers nerves that affect your focus and energy levels. Learning to calm your mind and channel that nervous energy into focus is a key skill for any cyclist.

Negative Self-Talk

Every cyclist has experienced the voice of self-doubt: I can't do this. I'm too slow. Everyone else is stronger than me. This internal dialogue can derail your ride if left unchecked. Developing positive mental habits can transform these thoughts into a powerful source of motivation.

Maintaining Focus on Long Rides

Cycling isn't just physically demanding—it's a test of mental endurance. Staying present and focused for hours at a time, especially when dealing with repetitive efforts or monotonous terrain, can be exhausting. Mental training helps you stay locked into the moment and maintain your edge.

How This Book is Structured

This book isn't about theory—it's a practical, step-by-step guide designed to make self-hypnosis an accessible and effective tool for cyclists of all levels. Whether you're completely new to mental training or already have some experience, this book will guide you through the process in a way that's easy to follow and apply.

1. **Starting with the Basics**

We'll begin by breaking down the fundamentals of self-hypnosis. You'll learn what it is, how it works, and why it's such a powerful tool for athletes. We'll explore the science behind hypnosis, including how it affects your subconscious mind, brainwaves, and habits. By the end of these chapters, you'll have a solid foundation to build on.

2. Building Your Skills

Once you understand the basics, we'll dive into the techniques. You'll learn how to enter a hypnotic state, create affirmations that resonate with your goals, and visualize success in vivid detail. These practical tools are designed to help you reframe negative thoughts, enhance your focus, and build resilience.

3. Putting It into Action

This section is all about real-world application. You'll discover how to use self-hypnosis to tackle specific cycling challenges, such as calming pre-race nerves, staying motivated on long rides, and managing pain during tough efforts. Each chapter will walk you through scenarios you're likely to encounter, showing you how to apply these techniques on the bike.

4. Pushing the Limits with Advanced Techniques

For those looking to take their mental game to the next level, we'll explore advanced techniques like accessing flow states, developing alert hypnosis (yes, you can hypnotize yourself while riding), and using hypnosis for long-term growth. These are the tools that elite athletes use to perform under pressure—and now, they'll be part of your toolkit too.

5. Making It a Lifestyle

In the final section, we'll focus on integrating self-hypnosis into your daily life. You'll learn how to make mental training a habit, align it with your physical workouts, and even use these tools outside of cycling—whether it's at work, in relationships, or in other areas of personal growth.

What You'll Gain

By the time you finish this book, you won't just be a stronger cyclist—you'll have a stronger mind. You'll know how to stay calm under pressure, reframe pain as progress, and push through mental barriers to unlock your true potential.

This isn't just about cycling—it's about developing a mindset that serves you in every area of life. The confidence, focus, and resilience you build here will ripple into everything you do.

Before We Start

Before we begin it's important to plant some seeds about mindset, our realities and how we experience them, and also how to approach the skills and knowledge within this book.

Don't worry, this isn't going to be 'Woo Woo' and as you'll learn within this book, hypnosis and self-hypnosis is just another tool within neuroscience, similar to mindfulness and mediation except self-hypnosis is used for creating a significant and massively powerful change in how we do or experience something.

Reality

'Reality', or our own personal realities are essentially how we 'experience' the world around us, how that world happens 'to' us, how we operate in that world and what those experiences teach us. What is important to begin to factor into your journey into learning self-hypnosis, and into life in general perhaps, is that reality is completely subjective and also elastic. How two people experience and interpret the same situation will be completely different based on their outlook, previous experiences and how they 'choose' to experience it.

We've all had one of 'those' rides which are just miserable right? It was freezing cold, and you couldn't feel your hands or feet (let alone your nose and ears!), you didn't get your fueling right and bonked, you'd maybe gone a bit hard too early. Maybe that was one of the worst experiences you've had on a bike? How did you experience that time? Was it a challenge, or was it an ordeal?

Sometimes taking conscious control over something that can often be habit, or an unconscious reaction can be all it takes to shift something from an ordeal to a challenge. Maybe it is forcing yourself to laugh out loud at the ridiculousness of the situation, or just focusing on the fact that you're in the middle of a ride which, in just a few hours, you'll be looking back on and smiling because let's face it, the joy of riding our bikes is why we do this right?

I guess, what I'm really trying to impart on you as we start this journey, is that how you experience things up to now doesn't have to be the 'default' and as you start to take these amazing steps to taking control over your mindset, especially conscious control over responses and experiences which may be unconscious until now, let yourself be completely open to the concept that you can chose to experience things differently.

Time

Yes, there's a whole book here to read and skills to learn, but many of the skills which you're going to learn, especially when starting out, are very short timewise and can easily be slotted in somewhere during your week. The initial sessions you do will probably be no longer than 5-10 minutes and if you can find a way to fit three or so of these in per week you'll see great results.

I've taught people these skills who then went on to do their 'off bike' self-hypnosis sessions on a bus or train while commuting to work, in bed before going to sleep, or even while sat in front of the TV while their family were watching something.

Fun!

Yes fun! Some of the techniques you will learn in this book started out as me just playing with my mind on my turbo trainer. For example, the 'Pain Net' visualization that you will learn to manage pain or discomfort started because before one of my turbo sessions I had been clearing out some old medical textbooks that contained those old hand-drawn medical illustrations. I saw an illustration of the nerve pathways on a page before my session and it reminded me of how pain is transmitted to the brain and during my workout I used the visualization and noticed in my legs that there was a difference.

All the things that you will learn in this book are tested, proven techniques that pretty much every cyclist who has learnt them has has benefitted from. Despite this there's a but..... pretty much every cyclist who has learnt that has benefitted from, **BUT** you might come up with something even more amazing which works for you. It's so important to treat these skills you will learn in a playful manner. Try different things. All the techniques you learn are underpinned by two things. Language and imagination. Play with them and see what you can do!

One cyclist I worked with took the well-known concept of burning matches when pushing hard to a whole new level and visualized actual matches burning when he was attacking or climbing...except his matchbox never ran out of matches!

Look for the Differences

This is really important and when you REALLY start to take notice things that are different and what has changed, it becomes very powerful and also builds even more on the ability to choose how to experience things. So what do I mean? Well, let's say you suffer from pre-event nerves and use the skills and techniques in this book to work on that.

The most common factor I see among people who do not get great results initially is that they focus on the core issue instead of noticing any improvements. Sure, you might still get nervous before an event, but what has changed? Did you feel more confident that previously? Only by beginning to look at what has changed will that change really begin to happen. What do you think is going to be more powerful to tell yourself, "I'm still nervous" or "I feeling more positive than before"? Out of ten were you less nervous than previously?

Also when you start to notice the changes that using these skills has created, that is when the changes can begin to snowball as you now know that change is achievable.

Ok, so let's begin this journey as you learn powerful techniques that will not only transform your cycling but can also be applied to everyday life.

2 THE HISTORY OF SELF HYPNOSIS

Hypnosis and its self-directed counterpart, self-hypnosis, have a long and fascinating history. From ancient rituals to modern sports psychology, the concept of altering consciousness to influence the mind and body has captivated humans for centuries. This chapter takes you through the key figures, eras, and breakthroughs that shaped self-hypnosis into the powerful tool it is today.

Ancient Beginnings (Circa 3000 BCE)

The roots of hypnosis can be traced back to ancient civilizations, where altered states of consciousness were a cornerstone of healing practices and rituals. In ancient Egypt, priests performed sleep temples, where individuals sought divine healing by entering trance-like states. Similarly, the Greeks adopted similar practices at the Temple of Asclepius, where patients experienced therapeutic dreams to address their ailments and this was also adopted by Romans who borrowed the concept of sleep healing. The word 'hypno' came from the Greek word for sleep 'hypnos' because from the outside, someone in hypnosis/doing self-hypnosis may appear asleep.

In these early contexts, hypnosis-like states were seen as mystical rather than psychological, often attributed to divine intervention. While there was no formal understanding of the subconscious mind, the idea that altered states could influence well-being laid the groundwork for future exploration.

Franz Mesmer and Mesmerism (18th Century)

In the late 18th century, Austrian physician Franz Anton Mesmer brought hypnosis into the medical realm. Mesmer believed in the concept of "animal magnetism," a universal fluid that could be manipulated to heal physical and psychological ailments. While his theories were later debunked, his methods of inducing trances—using rhythmic movements, eye fixation, and suggestion—captured the imagination of both physicians and the public.

Mesmer's work may not have been scientifically sound, but it marked a significant step toward understanding hypnosis as a repeatable process. His techniques laid the foundation for others to study hypnosis in a more structured and evidence-based way.

James Braid and the Birth of Hypnosis (1840s)

Scottish surgeon James Braid is credited with coining the term "hypnosis" (from the Greek word hypnos, meaning sleep) in the mid-19th century. Braid observed that focused attention and suggestion could produce a trance-like state, which he initially thought was a form of sleep. However, he later recognized that hypnosis was a unique state of consciousness, distinct from sleep.

Braid's work marked a departure from the mysticism of Mesmerism, grounding hypnosis in observation and experimentation. He also introduced self-hypnosis, teaching individuals to guide themselves into a hypnotic state for therapeutic purposes. This innovation paved the way for the use of hypnosis as a tool for personal empowerment.

Emile Coué and the Power of Suggestion (Early 20th Century)

French psychologist Emile Coué revolutionized self-hypnosis by emphasizing the power of suggestion. Coué believed that positive affirmations could reprogram the subconscious mind, leading to profound changes in behavior and well-being. His famous mantra, "Every day, in every way, I am getting better and better," became a cornerstone of self-hypnosis practice.

"We possess within us a force of incalculable power, which, when we handle it unconsciously is often prejudicial to us. If on the contrary we direct it in a conscious and wise manner, it gives us the mastery of ourselves and allows us not only to escape … from physical and mental ills, but also to live in relative happiness, whatever the conditions in which we may find ourselves." (Coue, 1922)

Coué's approach was simple yet highly effective, making self-hypnosis accessible to a wider audience. His work demonstrated that individuals could influence their mental and physical states through repetition and belief, concepts that remain central to self-hypnosis today.

The Rise of Clinical Hypnosis (Mid-20th Century)

In the mid-1900s, hypnosis gained credibility as a psychological and therapeutic tool. Figures like Milton Erickson, an American psychiatrist, transformed the practice by introducing a more flexible, individualized approach. Erickson viewed hypnosis not as a rigid process but as a way to tap into the natural suggestibility and creativity of the mind.

Erickson's techniques, which included storytelling and indirect suggestions, influenced modern therapeutic hypnosis and self-hypnosis methods. His work highlighted the subconscious mind's ability to solve problems and foster change when approached with subtlety and creativity.

Self-Hypnosis in Sports and Performance (Late 20th Century)

By the late 20th century, hypnosis had made its way into the world of sports. Athletes began using self-hypnosis to enhance focus, manage stress, and visualize success. Studies showed that mental rehearsal through hypnosis could improve muscle memory, reaction time, and performance consistency.

Olympians and world champions embraced these techniques to gain a mental edge. For example, many track and field athletes used visualization under hypnosis to mentally practice their events, enhancing their confidence and execution on the day of competition.

The Modern Era: Science and Accessibility (21st Century)

Today, self-hypnosis is recognized as a legitimate tool for personal and professional growth, backed by scientific research in neuroscience and psychology. Advances in brain imaging have shown that hypnosis alters brain activity, particularly in areas related to focus, pain perception, and emotional regulation.

Self-hypnosis is no longer confined to therapy or elite

performance; it has become a practical, everyday tool for managing stress, improving focus, and achieving goals. Apps, online courses, and books have made the practice accessible to anyone, including cyclists looking to enhance their mental game.

Why Self-Hypnosis Matters for Cyclists

The history of self-hypnosis is a story of discovery, adaptation, and empowerment. From ancient healing rituals to modern sports psychology, the practice has evolved into a scientifically validated method for unlocking the power of the mind. For cyclists, self-hypnosis offers a unique opportunity to tackle the mental challenges of the sport, whether it's managing pain, staying focused, or building confidence.

By understanding the rich history of self-hypnosis, you're not just learning a technique—you're stepping into a tradition that has helped people achieve extraordinary things for centuries. And now, it's your turn to carry that tradition forward, both on and off the bike.

3 THE SCIENCE OF SELF HYPNOSIS

Self-hypnosis is often misunderstood as a mysterious or mystical practice, but its power lies in something far more tangible: science. Grounded in neuroscience and psychology, self-hypnosis is a tool that allows you to tap into the brain's incredible adaptability and reprogram mental patterns that influence your thoughts, emotions, and performance. In this chapter, we'll explore the fascinating mechanisms behind self-hypnosis, from the relationship between the conscious and subconscious mind to the role of brainwave states, neuroplasticity, and its application in pain management.

The Relationship Between the Conscious and Subconscious Mind

To understand how self-hypnosis works, we first need to delve into the relationship between the two main players in your mind: the conscious and subconscious. These two systems work together to shape your behavior, but they play very different roles.

The Conscious Mind: Your Rational Navigator

The conscious mind is the part of your brain that you're actively aware of. It's responsible for logical thinking, decision-making, and analyzing your surroundings. When you're deciding whether to push harder on a climb or conserve energy for the descent, that's your conscious mind at work.

However, the conscious mind has limitations. It can only process a small amount of information at any given time, which is why it often feels overwhelmed under pressure. This is also the part of your brain that engages in self-doubt or overanalyzing—those *What if I'm not strong enough?* thoughts that can creep in during a tough ride.

The Subconscious Mind: Your Silent Powerhouse

If the conscious mind is the captain of the ship, the subconscious mind is the engine room. It operates behind the scenes, managing automatic processes like habits, emotional responses, and ingrained beliefs. For example, when you're pedaling, balancing, and shifting gears without thinking about it, that's your subconscious mind in action.

The subconscious doesn't analyze or question—it simply runs the programs it has learned over time. This is why negative thought patterns, such as I'm not good enough for this climb, can persist even when your conscious mind tries to override them with logic.

How the Two Work Together (or Against Each Other)

The conscious mind accesses the "library" of beliefs stored in the subconscious. If your subconscious is filled with empowering beliefs like I am strong and capable, your conscious mind can draw on those resources in moments of challenge. But if your subconscious is cluttered with negative scripts like I've failed at this before, those beliefs will influence your actions, often without you realizing it.

Self-hypnosis serves as a bridge between the conscious and subconscious mind. By quieting the analytical conscious mind, self-hypnosis allows you to communicate directly with the subconscious and replace unhelpful patterns with empowering ones.

Hypnosis and Brainwave States: Unlocking the Door to Focus and Creativity

Your brain is an orchestra of electrical activity, with different frequencies of brainwaves influencing your mental state. Understanding how hypnosis interacts with these brainwaves can help you unlock deeper focus, creativity, and resilience.

The Brain's Rhythm: What Are Brainwaves?

Your brain operates across several types of brainwaves, each associated with a specific mental state:

- Gamma Waves: The fastest brainwaves, linked to peak focus and problem-solving.

- **Beta Waves**: Active during normal waking states, when you're thinking critically or solving problems.

- **Alpha Waves**: Associated with relaxation and creativity, often referred to as the "gateway" to the subconscious.

- **Theta Waves**: A deeply meditative state where imagination and intuition thrive.

- **Delta Waves**: Dominant during deep sleep and physical recovery.

In self-hypnosis, the focus is on the Alpha and Theta states. These are the brainwaves that allow you to bypass your inner critic and engage directly with the subconscious.

Alpha Waves: The Calm Yet Focused State

Alpha brainwaves occur when your mind is calm yet alert. This state is ideal for relaxation, problem-solving, and creativity. During self-hypnosis, Alpha waves help you quiet the noise of self-doubt, making your mind more receptive to positive suggestions. For cyclists, Alpha waves can be especially useful for pre-ride visualization, calming nerves, and setting a focused intention.

Theta Waves: The Gateway to the Subconscious

Theta waves are slower than Alpha waves and are associated with deep relaxation and daydreaming. In this state, the subconscious mind becomes highly receptive to change. Hypnosis naturally guides your brain into Theta, allowing you to reprogram limiting beliefs, overcome mental barriers, and access your imagination.

For example, during a long, rhythmic ride, you may naturally enter a Theta-like state where repetitive motion and focus create a meditative experience. This is why some of your best ideas or moments of clarity often happen on the bike.

Neuroplasticity: Rewiring the Brain for Better Performance

One of the most exciting discoveries in neuroscience is the concept of neuroplasticity, which refers to the brain's ability to adapt and form new neural connections throughout life. Every time you repeat a thought, behavior, or belief, you're strengthening specific neural pathways, much like carving a trail through a forest.

How Neural Pathways Shape Habits and Beliefs

- Repetition Builds Strength: The more you repeat a thought (e.g., I'm terrible at sprints), the stronger that neural pathway becomes.

- Default Patterns: Over time, these pathways become automatic. Negative beliefs can feel "hardwired" because your brain has simply practiced them more often.

How Hypnosis Facilitates Change

Hypnosis leverages neuroplasticity by disrupting old, unhelpful pathways and creating new ones:

- Interrupting Negative Loops: Hypnosis helps you pause automatic negative thoughts, creating space for new beliefs.

- Strengthening Positive Connections: By visualizing success and repeating affirmations, you actively build new neural pathways that support your goals.

For example, if you've always thought, I'm not good at climbs, hypnosis can help you replace that belief with Every climb makes me stronger. With repetition, this new belief becomes your brain's default pattern or at least tipping the scales in your favor for it to happen more often than before.

Hypnosis for Pain Management: A Proven Tool

Pain is an inevitable part of cycling, whether it's the burn of a steep climb or the discomfort of hours in the saddle. But pain isn't just a physical sensation—it's also a mental experience, shaped by how your brain interprets and reacts to it. This is where self-hypnosis can be a game-changer.

The Science of Pain and Hypnosis

Clinical studies have consistently shown that hypnosis is an effective tool for managing pain. Research has demonstrated that hypnosis can:

- Reduce activity in the brain's pain-processing centers, such as the anterior cingulate cortex and somatosensory cortex.

- Alter the emotional response to pain, making it feel less overwhelming.

- Increase the brain's production of natural painkillers, such as endorphins.

These findings are backed by decades of clinical trials, showing that hypnosis can reduce chronic pain, post-surgical pain, and even labor pain. For athletes, this means that hypnosis can help you reframe pain as a manageable sensation rather than a limiting factor.

How Self-Hypnosis Helps Cyclists Manage Pain

Self-hypnosis allows you to shift your focus and change your perception of pain. Here's how:

1. Reframing Pain as Progress: Instead of interpreting pain as a signal to stop, hypnosis helps you reframe it as evidence of your effort and growth. For example, you might tell yourself, This burn in my legs in speed and power entering them, and perhaps try some visualization of a power entering your legs.

2. Dialing Down Discomfort: In a hypnotic state, you can use visualization techniques to "dial down" the intensity of pain. Imagine a volume knob in your mind, and picture yourself turning it down to a more manageable level, you'll learn this in more detail later.

3. Focusing Elsewhere: Hypnosis teaches you to shift your attention away from pain and onto other sensations, such as your breathing, cadence, or the rhythm of your pedaling.

Practical Applications During Rides

During a tough ride, you can use self-hypnosis techniques to manage pain in real time:

•	Breathing Focus: Sync your breath with your pedal strokes while repeating a calming affirmation, like I am strong and steady.

•	Visualization: Picture yourself cresting the hill with ease, feeling powerful and in control.

•	Anchoring: Create a mental "anchor," such as a calming word or image, that helps you quickly return to a state of focus and composure.

Bringing It All Together: The Science in Action

Self-hypnosis is not magic—it's neuroscience in motion. By understanding the interplay between your conscious and subconscious mind, leveraging brainwave states, tapping into neuroplasticity, and using proven pain management techniques, you can rewire your brain to support your cycling goals.

In the next chapters, we'll dive deeper into practical techniques for using self-hypnosis to build confidence, overcome challenges, and unlock your potential. Whether you're visualizing a strong climb, calming pre-race nerves, or reframing pain as progress, the science of self-hypnosis provides the foundation for meaningful change. Let's put these principles into action and see what your mind—and body—can truly achieve.

4. REAL LIFE CASE STUDIES

Mental training and visualization techniques have long been a staple in the arsenal of top athletes, including world-class cyclists. Legends like Sir Chris Hoy, a six-time Olympic gold medallist, have openly credited visualization as a key component of their success. Hoy described imagining every detail of his races—from the roar of the crowd to the feel of the bike beneath him—allowing him to rehearse success and stay calm under pressure.

Similarly, Tour de France champions like Chris Froome have incorporated mental techniques like visualization to handle the gruelling demands of long stages, overcome pain, and maintain focus. These tools enable elite athletes to tap into their subconscious minds, boosting confidence and resilience in high-stakes situations.

But these techniques aren't reserved for professionals. Cyclists and triathletes at all levels have unlocked their potential by integrating self-hypnosis, visualization, and other mental strategies. At Hypno Velo, I've seen remarkable transformations in cyclists from diverse backgrounds. Here are some of their stories:

1. Achieving Podium Success in Triathlon

R, a dedicated triathlete from the UK, sought to push his limits in preparation for an important event. He focused on integrating visualization techniques to address his most challenging segments of the race. By mentally rehearsing smooth transitions, steady pacing, and strong finishes, he developed the confidence to execute his plan under pressure.

On race day, he faced a tough second run but relied on the mental strategies he had practiced. Visualization allowed him to stay focused and composed, and also to dig deeper, ultimately leading to a second-place finish in his category. This brought him closer to their goal of qualifying for the Team GB age group team. His story demonstrates how mental preparation can transform training into tangible results.

2. Elevating Performance with Visualization

A veteran racer and member of a Women's Racing Team in USA came to Hypno Velo looking for an edge in their cycling performance. She struggled with maintaining motivation and focus during the most gruelling segments of training and racing, particularly on steep climbs.

Through one session focused on visualization, she learned to imagine their body working effortlessly through challenging efforts. This mental rehearsal reduced their perception of difficulty, allowing them to tackle steep climbs with more composure and less physical strain. By practicing visualization, she discovered a new mental approach to climbing that improved both their performance and confidence.

3. Overcoming Anxiety on Descents

I, a high-level racer from California, faced a mental roadblock after a near-collision with a car during a descent. The traumatic experience shook his confidence and he would be braking continually and crawling all the way down a descent.

By working through targeted mental strategies, he used self-hypnosis and visualization to rebuild their trust in their abilities. They visualized themselves descending smoothly, feeling in control and confident as they navigated familiar routes. He made some astonishing improvements in just a short amount of time.

On familiar courses, a few deep breaths at the top of a descent were enough to re-centre and refocus. He now uses visualization regularly both on and off the bike to maximise his performance. He was kind enough to share a video about his story which you can see on my website at www.hypnovelo.com if you'd like to hear from I himself.

4. Building Confidence in Competitive Racing

D, a Category 3 criterium racer, struggled with self-doubt and anxiety about their abilities, particularly regarding cornering in technical crit races. Although initially sceptical about hypnotherapy, she decided to explore mental training to enhance their performance in high-pressure situations.

Through guided self-hypnosis sessions with me, she developed affirmations and visualizations to combat their inner critic. During a particularly challenging time trial, she applied these techniques in real time. When overtaken by faster riders, instead of feeling defeated, she refocused on their own effort and goals, using affirmations like "I am strong and steady." The result was a performance that exceeded their expectations, proving that mental resilience can make the difference between giving up and achieving personal bests.

5. Unlocking Flow in Group Rides

Group rides can be intimidating, especially for newer riders or those returning from injury. M, a recreational cyclist, felt overwhelmed by the fast pace and competitive atmosphere of their local group rides. They often found themselves struggling to keep up, leading to frustration and feelings of inadequacy.

Through self-hypnosis, she practiced visualization exercises to prepare for group rides. She imagined herself drafting efficiently, holding a strong cadence, and staying calm under pressure. By mentally rehearsing these scenarios, she entered group rides with a sense of confidence and control. Over time, her performance improved, and they even found themselves enjoying the camaraderie and challenge of riding with others.

6. Managing Pain and Discomfort

T, a long-distance cyclist training for a multi-day event, used visualization to manage physical discomfort and effort during long rides. He practiced imagining a "dial" he could turn down to reduce the intensity of pain and also used the same dial to dial down his perceived effort during times when he was struggling.

Conclusion: Real Results Through Mental Training

From overcoming fear to reaching the podium, these real-life stories illustrate the transformative power of mental tools like self-hypnosis and visualization. Whether you're managing pre-race nerves, building confidence, or pushing through pain, these techniques provide practical solutions for the unique challenges cyclists face.

If these cyclists can unlock their potential through mental training, so can you. As you progress through the book, remember that every challenge is an opportunity to grow. By integrating these strategies into your cycling routine, you'll develop the mental edge to achieve your goals and enjoy the journey. The road ahead is yours—ride it with confidence.

5 'DOING' SELF HYPNOSIS: OVERVIEW

Mastering Self-Hypnosis: An Introduction to the Process

Self-hypnosis is one of the most transformative tools you can add to your mental training arsenal as a cyclist. It's a skill that allows you to tap into your subconscious mind, reframe unhelpful thought patterns, and unlock your true potential—both on and off the bike. But what exactly does self-hypnosis look like in practice, and how can it fit into your cycling routine? That's what this chapter is all about.

Think of this as your roadmap to mastering self-hypnosis. While we won't dive into the nitty-gritty details of each step just yet (that's coming in the following chapters), this chapter provides an overview of the process and what you can expect to learn. By the end of this book, you'll not only understand how to practice relaxed self-hypnosis in quiet moments but also how to use alert hypnosis while cycling to manage pain, enhance focus, and even access flow states.

Two Modes of Self-Hypnosis

Before we outline the steps, it's essential to understand the two main ways self-hypnosis can be practiced. Both have their unique benefits, and each serves different purposes depending on your goals and circumstances.

Relaxed Self-Hypnosis

This is the more traditional form of self-hypnosis, where you guide yourself into a deeply calm and focused state. Relaxed hypnosis is perfect for moments off the bike, such as before a race or during recovery. In this mode, you'll have the time and mental space to visualize your goals, embed affirmations, and work on reframing unhelpful mental patterns.
Relaxed self-hypnosis is ideal for:

- Calming pre-race nerves.

- Building confidence and resilience.

- Visualizing specific goals, like conquering a challenging climb or finishing strong in a race.

Alert Self-Hypnosis

Unlike relaxed hypnosis, alert self-hypnosis happens in motion. You can use it while cycling, staying fully aware of your surroundings as you guide your mental focus. This mode is perfect for real-time challenges, like managing pain during a climb, digging deep for extra effort, or staying in the zone during a long ride. Alert hypnosis is a powerful tool that can help you perform at your best in the moment.

Alert self-hypnosis is ideal for:

- Pain management during intense efforts.

- Sustaining focus and rhythm on long rides.

- Accessing flow states for peak performance.

In the chapters ahead, you'll learn how to master both modes, tailoring each to your cycling needs.

The Steps of Self-Hypnosis: A Bird's Eye View

Self-hypnosis isn't a one-size-fits-all process, but it does follow a general structure. Here's a quick overview of what the process involves, with the promise that we'll cover each step in detail in subsequent chapters.

Step 1: Setting Your Intention

Every self-hypnosis session begins with a clear goal. What do you want to achieve? Whether it's staying calm before a big race or managing discomfort during a tough ride, your intention is the compass that guides the entire process.

For example:

- Relaxed self-hypnosis intention: "I want to visualize myself finishing a race with confidence and strength."

- Alert self-hypnosis intention: "I want to stay focused and steady during this climb."

Step 2: Creating a Conducive Environment

To practice relaxed self-hypnosis you don't truly need a quiet, despite what 'traditional' hypnosis practitioners might advocate. In fact, as you build your self-hypnosis skillset the ability to go 'into' hypnosis in situations where there are background noises such as on your commute for example, will only help in the future when you're going to get into alert hypnosis on the bike and surrounded by distractions and sensory stimuli. Background noise can actually be used to help focus your attention. Ive hypnotised people with busy traffic sounds in the background including sirens and it really doesn't have any negative effect on the outcome.

However saying that, for your first steps into self-hypnosis you might find it useful to be somewhere quiet to start off.

For relaxed hypnosis:

- Find a quiet spot to sit or lie down comfortably.

- Eliminate distractions, such as your phone or background noise.

For alert hypnosis:

- Recognize your cycling environment as part of the practice.

- Use a technique like eye fixation and paying attention to your breathing will guide your attention and create that 'shift' of going into self-hypnosis (or flow).

Step 3: Entering a Focused State

In this step, you'll guide your mind from its usual busy, overthinking state into one of calm focus. Relaxation techniques, rhythmic breathing, and sensory engagement play a big role here.

Relaxed hypnosis techniques include:

- Deep breathing exercises to slow your heart rate and calm your mind.

- Progressive muscle relaxation to release tension in your body.

Alert hypnosis techniques include:

- Letting each outward breath guide your attention 'deeper' and more focused, quieting down your internal dialogue or chatter.

- Using the repetition of your pedal stroke as another source of taking your attending 'deeper'.

Step 4: Doing 'The Work'

This is where the real work happens. Once you're in a focused state, you can introduce affirmations or mental imagery to reshape your subconscious thoughts. For example:

- Relaxed hypnosis: Visualize yourself cresting a climb with ease while repeating affirmations like, "I am powerful and capable."

- Alert hypnosis: While riding, create internal visualizations while riding and also shape your language to suit your situation.

Step 5: Reinforcing and Exiting the State

Just as you entered hypnosis intentionally, you'll also exit it with purpose. This ensures that the benefits of the session stay with you as you move forward.

- Relaxed hypnosis: Gradually count yourself back to alertness, feeling calm and energized.

- Alert hypnosis: Transition from focused affirmations back to a broader awareness of your surroundings, carrying your positive mindset forward.

How This Book Will Guide You

The steps above might sound simple, but mastering self-hypnosis is a skill that, like any other skill you've learnt so far, takes practice and guidance—and that's exactly what the following chapters are here to provide. You'll learn how to refine your technique, overcome common challenges, and make self-hypnosis a natural part of your cycling routine.

Here's what's coming up:

- Relaxed Hypnosis Techniques: In the next chapters, we'll delve into the finer details of relaxed self-hypnosis. You'll learn how to create a calming environment, guide yourself into a hypnotic state, and use visualizations and affirmations to reprogram your mindset. These techniques are perfect for pre-ride preparation, recovery, and building long-term mental resilience.

- Alert Hypnosis on the Bike: Later, we'll focus on alert hypnosis, teaching you how to stay mentally sharp and focused while actively cycling. Whether you're managing pain on a tough climb, finding your flow state, or pushing through fatigue, these tools will become second nature with practice.

Conclusion: Your Journey Starts Here

Self-hypnosis is a skill that adapts to your needs and goals. Whether you're visualizing success in a relaxed state or staying focused during a ride, it's a tool that empowers you to unlock your full potential as a cyclist. This chapter has given you a glimpse of what's possible; now it's time to dig deeper into each step and make this practice your own.

With self-hypnosis in your toolkit, you'll discover that cycling isn't just about physical strength—it's about mastering the mental game. Let's get started!

6 'DOING' SELF HYPNOSIS: INDUCTION

Before diving into the depths of self-hypnosis, it's essential to establish a strong foundation—think of this as the "base training" phase of mental preparation, much like the work you do to build your aerobic capacity as a cyclist. Just as those long, steady rides lay the groundwork for explosive power later, practicing relaxed hypnosis provides the skills and mental discipline needed to master more advanced techniques like alert hypnosis, which you'll use on the bike for tasks like managing pain, accessing flow states, and pushing your performance boundaries.

This chapter will guide you through three effective induction techniques: Progressive Muscle Relaxation, Eye Fixation, and Countdown Induction. There are many, many different ways to 'enter' hypnosis, but these have been precisely chosen as the best methods for you as a cyclist and also with an eye towards you being to access these skills while active on the bike and just nailing these three techniques will provide you with everything you need. These methods are your entry point into self-hypnosis, allowing you to shift into a focused, receptive mental state where you can work with your subconscious mind. In addition, we'll address some common misconceptions about hypnosis to set your mind at ease. Finally, we'll explore the importance of a smooth "awakening" process to end your sessions on a positive, empowering note.

Debunking a Common Hypnosis Myth

Before we dive into the techniques, let's tackle one of the most pervasive misconceptions about hypnosis: the idea that you'll lose control or become "stuck" in a hypnotic state. Rest assured, that's not how hypnosis works.

At any time during self-hypnosis, you can simply open your eyes and return to full awareness. Hypnosis is a state of heightened focus and receptivity, not a trance-like loss of control. Sadly these unhelpful myths stem from stage hypnosis where some kind of powerful hypnotist takes control of their subjects which couldn't be further from the truth! You remain fully aware of your surroundings and entirely in charge of the process. It's much like daydreaming—you can choose to snap out of it whenever you want. The way I explain to people I'm working with one to one in direct hypnosis is that I may have the map but they're the ones driving the car.

Throughout this chapter, you'll see that hypnosis is a flexible, empowering tool. Whether you're practicing in a relaxed setting or on the bike, you're always in control, and the process is entirely in your hands.

Progressive Muscle Relaxation: Your Gateway to Hypnosis

What It Is

Progressive Muscle Relaxation (PMR) is one of the most popular and effective induction techniques, especially for beginners. It involves systematically relaxing each muscle group in your body, helping you transition into a state of calm and focus. It's an excellent starting point for building your hypnosis skills and creating a strong mental foundation.

How It Works

PMR works by redirecting your focus from external distractions to the sensations in your body. By consciously releasing physical tension, you simultaneously quiet your mind, allowing you to shift into a receptive, hypnotic state.

Step-by-Step Guide to Progressive Muscle Relaxation

1. Find a Comfortable Position

• Sit or lie down in a quiet, comfortable space where you won't be disturbed. Close your eyes and take a few deep breaths to settle yourself. Let yourself take one big deep breath in, then breath out deeply and strongly and let that breath begin to take to into a more focused state. Do it the same as someone would about to swim underwater except instead on holding breath. Let it go.

2. Start with Your Head

• Focus on your head. Allow yourself to experience the sensation of any tension draining down from your head, down your face, into your neck, replacing the tension with a lovely, perhaps warm, relaxation.

3. Work Your Way Down

• Gradually move through each muscle group: your shoulders, arms, wrists. Then your chest, abdomen, thighs, then calves and then feet. For each group:

- Allow the sensation of tension leaving each muscle, draining down through your feet or body, into the couch or floor.

- Let a warm, deeply relaxed sensation replace any tension in any muscle and let yourself become more deeply focused with each body part and each breath.

4. Combine with Visualization

- As you release tension, imagine in any way that suits you, tension draining down and away out of your body.

5. Doing 'The Work'

- Once your body feels relaxed, shift your attention to your suggestions or visualizations. Your mind is now in the ideal state to do the work.

When to Use PMR

- Pre-Ride Preparation: Calm your nerves and focus on your goals.

- Post-Ride Recovery: Release tension and promote relaxation after a tough session.

- General Relaxation: Use PMR anytime you need to reset and recharge.

Eye Fixation: Sharpening Your Focus

What It Is

Eye Fixation is a focused induction technique that helps you develop mental discipline and concentration. By training your mind to stay engaged with a single point, Eye Fixation prepares you for alert hypnosis—a skill you'll use during turbo trainer sessions, challenging climbs, long rides and races.

How It Works

Unlike PMR, which emphasizes relaxation, Eye Fixation sharpens your focus and builds your ability to maintain mental clarity. This technique is particularly useful for cyclists who want to stay engaged during repetitive efforts or intense moments.

Step-by-Step Guide to Eye Fixation

1. Choose a Fixed Point

- Select an object or area to focus on such as a spot on the wall straight ahead. This works great if you are on your turbo trainer and also builds the foundation for being able to into this state while actually riding and taking in the road ahead.

Other good option is just looking down at a spot on the back your hand if you're not on your bike (great for practising going in and out of hypnosis quickly while on a bus or waiting for a meeting).

    2.   Relax Your Gaze and facial muscles

- Stare at the chosen point with a soft, relaxed focus. Let your peripheral vision blur slightly as your thoughts begin to settle. Let your face become slack and relaxed.

    3.   Engage Your Breathing

- With each deep, outward breath, let your attention become more focused. As you progress you will notice a 'shift' in your attention. Everything inside becomes 'quieter'. Some people notice a change in sensation somewhere in their body.

4.   Close Your Eyes (Skip this part if doing active hypnosis, just go straight to 'Doing the Work')

- Once you have noticed a 'shift' in your attention, continue the eye fixation until you just feel like you want to allow your eyes to close.

    5.   Doing 'The Work'

- When ready (you can give yourself a period of relaxation or letting go of any tension during this time if you wish) now go ahead with the suggestions and/or visualization.

5. Maintaining Hypnosis

- If doing alert hypnosis, it can be difficult to remain 'in' hypnosis for long periods of time, especially when starting out. The amount of time you can maintain the state will get longer with practice but also there may be periods of time on the bike where it seem natural to drift out, but when you want to start again just do a couple of deep in and out breaths and then exhale deeply and let that take you back into it.

When to Use Eye Fixation

- Turbo Trainer Sessions: Stay focused during intervals or repetitive efforts.

- Pre-Race Preparation: Use this technique to center yourself before the start line.

- Mid-Ride Performance: Maintain mental clarity during climbs or long stretches of road.

Countdown Induction: Guiding the Mind Into Focus

What It Is

Countdown Induction is a simple, structured technique that helps you transition into a hypnotic state by combining focused breathing with mental imagery. By counting down from 10 to 1, you create a steady rhythm that calms your mind and sharpens your focus.

Step-by-Step Guide to Countdown Induction

1. Set the Scene

- Find a quiet space where you can sit or lie down comfortably. Close your eyes and take a few deep breaths.

2. Begin Counting Down

- Inhale deeply as you think or say the number 10, then exhale slowly, imagining yourself sinking deeper into relaxation. Tell yourself that with each number you will go into hypnosis more deeply.

- Continue this process, counting down with each breath: 9… 8… 7… until you reach 1.

3. Visualize the Descent

- With each number, picture yourself descending a staircase or sinking into a soft chair. Imagine yourself becoming calmer and more focused with every step.

4. Transition to Suggestions

- Once you've reached 1, introduce positive affirmations or visualizations that align with your goals.

When to Use Countdown Induction

- Pre-Ride Preparation: Use the countdown to calm your mind and focus your intentions.

- Post-Ride Recovery: Visualize your body recovering and growing stronger as you count down.

- Quick Resets: This technique is perfect for regaining focus and composure in any situation.

How Long Should Your Hypnosis Session Be?

When you first start building your hypnosis skills, you will probably only manage 5-10 minutes and they will probably feel a very long time! Keep track of how long your sessions are and aim to do longer sessions bit by bit, aiming for ideally 20-30 minutes.

A good way of keeping track of time is to set a gentle reminder on your phone or clock to let you know when you've reached the duration you are aiming for.

Awakening: Finishing Your Hypnosis Session

When your hypnosis session is complete, it's important to "awaken" in a way that reinforces the positive work you've done. Ending your session with intentionality helps you carry the benefits forward into your day or ride.

How to Awaken

1. Introduce Positive Suggestions

- Before opening your eyes, tell yourself:

- "I'm going to wake up feeling refreshed and confident."

- "I'll carry this calm focus into my ride."

2. Count Up to 10

- Just as you counted down during induction, you can count up to signal the end of your session.

- With each number, imagine yourself becoming more alert and energized. When you reach 10, open your eyes and stretch gently.

3. Take a Moment to Reflect

- Sit quietly for a moment and notice how you feel. Acknowledge any positive shifts in your focus, relaxation, or mindset.

What's Next?

In the following chapters, we'll explore how to deepen your practice and apply these induction techniques to real-world cycling scenarios. From managing pain and accessing flow states to building confidence and endurance, you'll learn how to tailor self-hypnosis to your unique goals.

Remember, the more you practice, the more natural and effective these techniques will become. So, let's keep building that mental base—your best rides are ahead!

7 'DOING' SELF HYPNOSIS: THE POWER OF LANGUAGE

The Power of Language: Unlocking the Subconscious Mind

The words we speak, think, and internalize hold immense power. They shape our perception of ourselves, influence our behaviours, and ultimately determine how we perform—both on and off the bike. In self-hypnosis, language becomes the key to unlocking the subconscious mind, allowing you to reprogram self-limiting beliefs and replace them with empowering, performance-enhancing thoughts.

When we talk about hypnosis suggestions, we're talking about the art of using language intentionally. The subconscious mind is highly suggestible, meaning it responds to repetition, vivid imagery, and positive phrasing. This is why crafting the right suggestions is so critical: they serve as the mental seeds you plant, nurture, and grow over time.

How Language Shapes the Subconscious Mind

THE CYCLIST'S MIND

To understand the power of language in hypnosis, we need to revisit the relationship between the conscious and subconscious mind. The conscious mind is analytical and critical—it filters and judges the words and thoughts we encounter. The subconscious mind, however, is like fertile soil: it absorbs whatever is planted in it without judgment. It doesn't differentiate between helpful or harmful suggestions; it simply accepts them and incorporates them into its programming.

Also language shapes how we experience things which in turn affects how our subconscious treats situations. Here's a quick exercise:

1. Close your eyes.
2. Tell yourself that you "Cant" do something and notice how that feels.
3. Now tell yourself that you "Could" do something and notice how the feeling gets lighter.
4. Now tell yourself that you "Can" do something and feel again the difference.

See how the language we use both on ourselves and also others affects how it shapes the experience?

The Role of Repetition

The subconscious mind learns through repetition. This is why we rehearse things to get them into our brains. Repeated self-talk—whether positive or negative—reinforces neural pathways in the brain. For example:

- "I always struggle on climbs" becomes a deeply ingrained belief if repeated often enough.

- "I become stronger with every climb I take" creates a completely different narrative, building confidence over time.

The Power of Positivity

The subconscious doesn't process negatives well. If you tell yourself, "Don't panic," the subconscious focuses on "panic." This is why hypnosis suggestions are always phrased in the positive. For example:

- Replace "I won't quit on tough climbs" with "I grow stronger with every climb."

Present Tense vs. Future Tense

The subconscious operates in the now. Suggestions like "I will be confident" imply confidence is something for the future—not now. Instead, frame suggestions as if they are already true: "I am confident and growing stronger every ride."

Hypnotic Language Loops: Suggestions That Keep Running

One of the most powerful tools in hypnosis is the use of language loops—phrases designed to remain active in the subconscious mind long after the session is over. These loops work by introducing open-ended ideas that suggest continuous improvement, reinforcing positive changes even when you're not consciously thinking about them.

Why Language Loops Work

Language loops capitalize on the brain's natural tendency to create patterns and seek improvement. By embedding suggestions that imply ongoing progress, you create a self-sustaining system of mental reinforcement.

Examples of Hypnotic Language Loops

- "Every time I climb a hill, I become stronger and more confident."

This loop links physical effort with mental growth, creating a positive association with climbing.

- "I am becoming more resilient with every setback"

This phrase suggests continuous progress, helping your subconscious see obstacles as opportunities to improve.

- "With every race I feel stronger, more confident and more focused."

This creates a connection between each race and positive mindset, making every race feel empowering.

Crafting Effective Hypnosis Suggestions

Creating powerful suggestions requires thought and precision. Here's a guide to crafting language loops that resonate deeply with your subconscious:

1. Keep It Positive

Focus on what you want to achieve, not what you want to avoid. For example:

- Use: "I grow stronger and more determined with every ride."

- Avoid: "I won't feel weak on this ride."

2. Be Specific

Vague suggestions like "I want to improve" don't provide clear direction. Instead, focus on specific outcomes:

- "Every time I push through discomfort, I build my endurance and strength."

3. Use Present Tense

Frame your suggestions as if the desired outcome is already happening:

- "I am becoming faster and more confident with every ride."

4. Create a Continuous Loop

Tie your suggestion to a recurring event or sensation, reinforcing the idea of ongoing improvement:

- "With each pedal stroke, I feel stronger, more balanced, and more capable."

Using Language Loops for Common Cycling Scenarios

Hypnotic language loops are particularly effective when tailored to the unique challenges cyclists face. Below are examples of language loops for specific scenarios, designed to keep running in the subconscious long after a hypnosis session:

1. Conquering Long Climbs

Long climbs can feel daunting, but language loops can transform them into opportunities for growth:

- "Every time I climb, my legs grow stronger, and my mind becomes sharper."

- "With every pedal stroke on this climb, I feel more capable and energized."

- "Each climb teaches me resilience and builds my confidence for the next."

2. Managing Pain and Discomfort

Pain is inevitable in cycling, but it doesn't have to derail your performance. Use these loops to reframe discomfort:

- "Each sensation of effort shows me I'm growing stronger and more powerful."

- "Every moment of discomfort is a sign that I'm achieving something great."

- "The more I ride through pain, the more I realize how capable I am."

3. Staying Calm Under Pressure

Pressure-filled moments—like race starts or tough competition—demand mental clarity. Use these loops to stay composed:

- "Every deep breath I take calms my nerves and focuses my mind."

- "With every race start, I grow more calm, confident, and prepared."

- "The more I face high-pressure moments, the more focused and steady I become."

4. Recovering from Setbacks

Setbacks, like crashes or missed goals, can impact confidence. Use these loops to build resilience:

- "Each setback teaches me valuable lessons and makes me stronger."

- "Every challenge I face builds my determination and shapes my success."

- "The more I recover from setbacks, the more unstoppable I become."

5. Achieving Flow States

Flow—the state of effortless focus—is a goal for many cyclists. These loops can help you access and maintain it:

- "Each time I ride, I become more in tune with my body and my bike."

- "With every pedal stroke, I sink deeper into focus and flow."

- "The more present I am, the more effortless my ride becomes."

6. Visualizing Success

Visualization primes the mind for achievement. Pair these loops with vivid mental imagery:

- "Each time I imagine success, I grow more confident and capable."

- "The more I see myself riding strong, the more natural it feels to perform that way."

- "Every visualization strengthens my ability to perform at my peak."

Awakening the Power of Language

The words you choose, especially during self-hypnosis, aren't just idle thoughts—they're the foundation of transformation. Hypnotic language loops work like a cycling training plan: they build strength, resilience, and focus over time, creating lasting changes in your mindset and performance.

Remember, the subconscious mind is always listening, and every repetition reinforces the beliefs and habits you want to cultivate. As you continue reading, you'll discover more ways to refine and expand your use of hypnotic suggestions, making them a powerful ally in every ride.

THE CYCLIST'S MIND

With practice, you'll not only reframe how you think about challenges but also experience a profound shift in how you approach cycling—and life. Let's keep moving forward!

8 VISUALIZATION

Visualization is one of the most powerful tools you can use to enhance your cycling performance. By creating vivid mental images, engaging your senses, and connecting emotionally with your goals, visualization allows you to mentally rehearse success before it happens. This isn't just about positive thinking; it's about training your brain and body to respond in ways that are more focused, confident, and capable. Whether you're preparing for a race, tackling a tough climb, or managing discomfort, visualization provides a powerful edge.

In this chapter, we'll begin by exploring how to incorporate visualization into your self-hypnosis practice, both in relaxed and alert states. Then, we'll introduce structured models of visualization, such as PETTLEP, to guide you in creating highly effective mental imagery. Finally, we'll dive into specific visualization techniques for common cycling scenarios, helping you prepare your mind and body for peak performance.

Incorporating Visualization Into Self-Hypnosis

Visualization and self-hypnosis go hand in hand. Once you've guided yourself into a hypnotic state using an induction technique, visualization becomes a natural next step. In this focused state, your subconscious mind is more receptive to the mental images you create, allowing those images to have a profound impact on your beliefs, confidence, and performance.

First or Third Person?

One of the questions often asked about visualization is whether to see yourself from a third person view, or see the scene unfold from your own perspective. I always tell people to just go with whatever feels natural to them. If you naturally seem to drift towards third person perspective and see yourself from the view of another, just roll with that but just make sure that you still feel all the sensations and emotions that go with what is happening.

Anecdotally, and completely unsupported by any scientific evidence, I feel that first person perspective is more effective. It's how we view things as we operate in our everyday lives so the images we present to our brains are more 'convincing' to our subconscious minds and also more like to create new patterns in our neurology.

Bit, as I mention, just go with what feels right for you. Don't try to force yourself into changing perspective.

How to Visualize in Relaxed Self-Hypnosis

1. Set the Scene: After your induction, clarify what you want to visualize. Are you mentally rehearsing a successful ride, building confidence for a race, sprinting more powerfully, cornering more confidently or preparing for a challenging climb?

2. Engage Your Senses: Visualization works best when it feels real. Imagine not only what you'll see but also what you'll hear, feel, smell, and even taste. The more vivid the experience, the more impactful it will be. Build the scene, feel the bar tape beneath your fingers, and the saddle underneath you. Hear the drivetrain of your bike and the wind in your ears.

3. Engage Your Senses: Visualization works best when it feels real. Imagine not only what you'll see but also what you'll hear, feel, smell, and even taste. The more vivid the experience, the more impactful it will be. Build the scene, feel the bar tape beneath your fingers, and the saddle underneath you. Hear the drivetrain of your bike, the wind in your ears. If you race, perhaps hear the crowd cheering you on.

4. Feel the Emotions: Your subconscious responds strongly to emotions, so connect with the feelings associated with your visualization. Whether it's pride, determination, or calmness, let those emotions flow through you. A great way of building emotion is noticing where in your body you feel that emotion and then grow it bigger and allow yourself to feel even more of that as it grows.

5. Visualize everything going the best possible way possible. Feel the emotions and sensations that you want to feel in the best situation possible. If practicing a practical aspect of cycling like cornering, run through that scene carrying out the best corner possible, feel how good that feels, feel the confidence and pride in doing that.

6. Repetition for Impact: Repeat the visualization a few times during your session, refining the details each time. Repetition helps strengthen the neural pathways associated with your goals.

Re-running Past Successes or Modelling Excellence

Ever had one of 'those' rides where everything was just amazing? Or where you nailed that sprint or climb as best as you could ever imagine? Use those memories to your advantage by replaying them in your mind as the first scene in your visualization. Let yourself experience the emotion that helped that performance, whether it was confidence or focus. Or maybe it was physical power that helped you sprint to first place or nail a climb.

Use that, let that feeling build in your body as the scene plays, let it build even bigger as the scene unfolds to completion. Then, while keeping that feeling inside your body, visualize a new, future scenario where that even bigger feeling leads to another successful outcome.

If you don't have anything like this to pull a memory from, well there are tons of professional cyclists out there from whom you can model excellence. Want to work on your sprinting but haven't had a win yet? Visualize role modelling excellence instead. Visualize being Cav sprinting down the Champs Elysee to a win. Feel the ability to hop from wheel to wheel with confidence and then feel the power to sprint past everyone for the win. Feel how amazing that would feel. And then, carry those sensations and feelings with you into your own, future scenario where you sprint for a win yourself. Have fun with it!

Visualization in Alert Hypnosis

Visualization isn't limited to relaxed states. You can use it during alert hypnosis, such as when riding or training. Just as you can imagine a conversation while walking or plan your day while driving, you can visualize success while cycling.

1. Choose Your Focus: While riding, decide on a specific visualization, like maintaining perfect form during a climb or staying calm during a sprint.

2. Layer it Onto Your Ride: Picture your mental image while staying aware of your surroundings. For example, as you pedal, imagine yourself cresting a hill with ease or nailing a smooth corner.

3. Embrace the Multitasking: Alert visualization doesn't require total immersion—just enough focus to guide your mindset while you ride.

4. Look Ahead: In later chapters, particularly the one on pain management, you'll learn how to use visualization in alert hypnosis to reduce perceived effort and discomfort.

Using Visualization Models: The PETTLEP Framework

To make your visualizations as effective as possible, you can use structured models like PETTLEP. This model was developed to enhance sports performance by ensuring visualizations closely replicate the real experience. PETTLEP stands for Physical, Environment, Task, Timing, Learning, Emotion, and Perspective. Let's break it down:

1. Physical

Incorporate physical actions or sensations into your visualization. If you're rehearsing a climb, imagine how your body feels as you grip the handlebars, push the pedals, and maintain your posture.

2. Environment

Visualize the actual setting where the performance will take place. Picture the road, the crowd, the weather, or the landmarks along the route.

3. Task

Focus on the specific task you're trying to improve. For instance, if it's sprinting, include the movements, gear shifts, and timing required to execute a perfect sprint.

4. Timing

Your visualization should match the real-time pace of the task. If climbing a hill typically takes 10 minutes, mentally rehearse it in real-time rather than fast-forwarding through it.

5. Learning

Adapt your visualization as you improve. If you're working on a technical skill like cornering, refine your mental image to match your growing proficiency.

6. Emotion

Engage the emotions you'll feel during the actual event. Whether it's determination, pride, or joy, let these emotions infuse your visualization.

7. Perspective

Choose between first-person (seeing the world through your eyes) or third-person (watching yourself perform). Use whichever perspective feels most natural, but ensure it evokes the desired emotions and sensations.

By following the PETTLEP framework if you wish, you ensure your visualizations are grounded in reality, making them more effective for improving performance and confidence.

Techniques for Specific Cycling Scenarios

Once you've mastered the basics of visualization, you can tailor it to specific challenges or goals. Each scenario below includes steps and examples to help you create powerful mental rehearsals.

1. Improving Specific Techniques

Visualization is a fantastic way to refine technical skills like cornering, pedalling efficiency, or bike handling. In self-hypnosis or alert states, mentally rehearse each aspect of the skill you want to improve.

1. Set Your Scene: Imagine a training session where you're focusing on a specific skill, like cornering or maintaining a steady cadence.

2. Engage Your Senses: Picture your posture, hear the rhythm of your breathing, and feel the smoothness of your movements. Feel the parts of your body doing exactly what they need to do to make the most perfect example of what you want to do. This also primes your nervous system to do this in real life.

3. Use a PETTLEP-Style Loop: Repeat a phrase like, "Every time I visualize this, my technique becomes smoother and more natural."

2. Sprinting: Unleashing Power

Sprinting requires a combination of explosive energy and mental focus. Visualization helps you rehearse staying composed and executing the perfect sprint.

1. Set the Stage: Picture the final stretch of a race, with the finish line in sight.

2. Feel the Effort: Imagine the tension in your legs and the controlled power as you accelerate.

3. Reinforce with a Loop: "With every sprint I visualize, I become faster, stronger, and more controlled."

3. Climbing: Conquering the Hills

Climbing challenges your mental and physical endurance. Visualization helps you approach climbs with determination and poise.

1. Imagine the Climb: Picture yourself on a steep gradient, maintaining a steady rhythm as you ascend.

2. Reframe the Effort: Visualize the burning in your legs as a sign of growing strength and progress.

3. Add a Loop: "Every climb I visualize builds my strength, confidence, and power."

4. Digging Deeper: Finding Reserves

When you're exhausted, visualization can help you tap into hidden energy reserves and push past your limits.

1. Picture Resilience: Imagine yourself riding through fatigue, finding strength with each pedal stroke.

2. Feel the Determination: Engage the emotion of pride and satisfaction, knowing you're giving your best.

3. Use a Loop: "Every time I dig deeper, I unlock more power and endurance."

5. Managing Pain: Reframing Discomfort

Visualization can change how you perceive pain, making it feel less overwhelming and easier to manage.

1. Shift the Focus: Imagine the pain fading into the background as you focus on your rhythm or the scenery around you.

2. Reframe the Sensation: Visualize discomfort as energy fueling your effort.

3. Add a Loop: "With every breath, I feel stronger, calmer, and more in control."

6. Pre-Event Mindset: Building Confidence

Visualization before an event prepares your mind for the challenges ahead and boosts your confidence.

1. Rehearse the Day: Imagine each stage of the event, from warming up to crossing the finish line.

2. Anticipate Obstacles: Picture how you'll handle challenges with calm determination.

3. Use a Loop: "Every time I prepare mentally, I feel more ready, focused, and confident."

Conclusion: Visualization as a Superpower

By following structured models like PETTLEP and tailoring your visualizations to specific cycling scenarios, you're not just preparing for success—you're creating it. The key to effective visualization lies in making it vivid, engaging all your senses, and connecting deeply with the emotions of achievement.

Practice these techniques regularly, and watch as they translate into better performance, greater confidence, and an unstoppable mindset on and off the bike. Let's keep riding toward mastery!

9. PAIN MANAGEMENT

Pain and discomfort are unavoidable parts of cycling, whether it's the burning in your legs during a climb, the ache in your lower back after hours in the saddle, or the fatigue creeping in during a long time trial. But what if you could reduce that pain—not eliminate it entirely, but lessen its impact—just enough to keep going when your body says stop?

Hypnosis and self-hypnosis have been extensively studied in clinical settings for their remarkable ability to reduce pain. From chronic conditions like fibromyalgia to acute surgical pain, hypnosis has consistently shown significant benefits in reducing perceived pain. If hypnosis can create measurable relief for people dealing with serious clinical pain, imagine what it could do for you on the bike. A 10% or 20% reduction in discomfort might be all you need to push through that climb or maintain focus during the final miles of a race.

Let's explore the science behind hypnosis and pain, and how you can apply these techniques to manage cycling discomfort, both in relaxed hypnosis and on the bike.

The Science of Hypnosis and Pain Reduction

Pain is not just a physical sensation—it's also a product of how the brain interprets signals from the body. When you feel pain, it's because receptors in your body send signals to the brain, which then processes and interprets those signals as discomfort. Hypnosis interrupts this process by altering the way the brain perceives and processes pain.

What Scientists Have Found

Research has shown that hypnosis can significantly reduce activity in the brain areas responsible for pain perception, such as the anterior cingulate cortex, somatosensory cortex, and insula. Here's what happens during hypnosis:

• Lowered Pain Sensitivity: Hypnosis decreases the brain's sensitivity to pain signals, making them feel less intense.

• Altered Emotional Response: Hypnosis changes how you emotionally react to pain, reducing feelings of distress or overwhelm associated with discomfort.

• Redirected Attention: Hypnosis helps shift focus away from pain and onto something else, whether it's your breathing, visualization, or a specific goal.

In cycling, where pain is often short-term but intense, these mechanisms can be incredibly effective. Even a modest reduction in discomfort can make the difference between finishing strong and giving up.

Pain Management Off the Bike: Relaxed Hypnosis Techniques

The best place to start learning pain management through hypnosis is off the bike, where you can practice techniques in a calm, controlled environment. These sessions allow you to experiment with visualization and mental rehearsal, so you're ready to apply the techniques when it matters most.

1. Dialing Down Pain

This technique involves imagining that pain is controlled by a dial or volume knob that you can adjust.

Steps:

1. Acknowledge the Pain: Accept the sensation rather than resisting it. Identify its location and intensity.

2. Visualize the Pain Dial: Imagine a large dial, similar to a volume control, representing your pain. The numbers range from 1 to 10, with 10 being maximum discomfort.

3. Turn the Dial Down: In your head, move the number into a lower number lowering the intensity of the pain, move it down by 1 or 2. Pair this with deep breaths. As you reduce the number really pay attention to the sensation in your legs and notice the difference.

4. Feel the Shift: As the number drops, notice how the sensation in your body changes. Picture the pain becoming duller, smaller, or more manageable.

5. Reinforce with Affirmations: Use affirmations to reinforce the shift, such as "Just a sensation"

6. You will find that as time passes, the number will drift back upwards. Every so often repeat the process and drop the number back down by 1 or 2.

2. The Pain Net Technique

This visualization technique helps you intercept pain signals before they reach your brain.

Steps:

1. Imagine the Pain Signals: Picture the pain signals as glowing blobs or sparks traveling from your legs, up toward your brain.

2. Visualize a Net: Imagine a strong, flexible net stretched through your body at your waist.

3. Catch the Signals: In your mind let yourself become aware of the net catching a lot of the blobs. As the pain blobs hit the net, visualize them sticking to it and dissipating, unable to reach your brain.

4. Focus on the Relief: As the net catches the signals, allow yourself to notice feel the sensation of the pain reducing.

5. Anchor the Feeling: Pair this visualization with a cue, such as clenching your handlebars, to reinforce the sensation of relief.

Using Time Distortion for Pain Management

Hypnosis can also help you manipulate your perception of time, which can be a game-changer in managing discomfort during long or intense efforts.

Speeding Up Time for Long Rides

1. **Imagine Time Accelerating:** Picture the ride as a highlight reel, where the miles pass quickly and effortlessly.

2. **Focus on Milestones:** Mentally jump from one milestone to the next, such as road markers or aid stations, imagining each coming sooner than expected.

3. **Reinforce with Affirmations:** Repeat statements like, "This ride passes with ease, and I feel strong every mile."

Conclusion: Reclaiming Control Over Pain

Pain is a natural part of cycling, but it doesn't have to control your performance. Through self-hypnosis and visualization, you can reframe discomfort, reduce its intensity, and push through challenges with greater ease. Whether you're practicing these techniques in a relaxed state or applying them mid-ride, the key is consistency and noticing what changes. Each time you use these tools, you're building your resilience and unlocking your potential to thrive under pressure.

THE CYCLIST'S MIND

Pain might be inevitable, but suffering is optional. With self-hypnosis, you can transform how you experience discomfort and take your cycling performance to new heights. Let's keep pedalling forward—stronger, calmer, and more in control.

THE CYCLIST'S MIND

10. The Robot

The Robot is such a powerful visualization for on the bike I just had to give it its own chapter! It really can be a game changer. This is a great technique for a range of race or ride situations, from digging deeper, reducing negative self-talk, sticking to certain goals or just getting into flow.

At its core, The Robot cyclist visualization is about simplifying your mental state by removing unnecessary emotions, overthinking, and self-doubt. It leverages the idea of detachment—not from your love of cycling, but from the distractions that hinder peak performance.

This is definitely one to have fun with. Imagine becoming The Terminator on a bike ruthlessly hunting down cyclists ahead of you, or just relentlessly powering through the miles.

The Psychology Behind The Robot

- **Emotional Detachment:** By imagining yourself as a robot, you take the emotion out of the equation. Nerves, self-doubt, and frustration are set aside, allowing you to focus purely on execution. Robots operates with a sole focus on achieving what is programmed into them.

•   **Precision and Efficiency:** Robots operate with smooth, flawless precision. Visualizing this reinforces your ability to execute techniques and strategies without hesitation or second-guessing.

•   **Accessing Flow:** Flow is often described as a state of being "in the zone," where actions feel effortless and time seems to warp. The Robot visualization helps quiet the inner critic, which is one of the primary barriers to achieving flow.

•   **Reducing Cognitive Overload:** By embodying The Robot mindset, you eliminate unnecessary internal dialogue, freeing up mental capacity for the ride itself.

The Benefits of The Robot

1. **Calm Under Pressure**

•   Emotional nerves before a race or during a challenging ride can drain your energy. By visualizing yourself as a robot, you bypass these emotions, staying calm and focused.

2. **Powerful**

- Robots don't tire. They just plough on ruthlessly, mile after mile, maintaining the pace they need to achieve their ultimate goal or mission.

3. **Reduced Negative Self-Talk**

- Robots don't indulge in self-criticism. Visualizing yourself as one can help you replace thoughts like "I can't do this" with neutral, task-focused thinking.

4. **Enhanced Precision and Technique**

- By imagining your movements as robotic, you reinforce efficient pedalling, smooth cornering, and other technical skills.

Using The Robot Visualization

1. Accessing Flow Through the Robot Cyclist

Flow states require full immersion in the present moment, free from distractions or self-consciousness. Visualizing yourself as a robot cyclist helps quiet the mental chatter that keeps you from entering this state.

Steps to Visualize:

1. **Pre-Ride Preparation:**

• Close your eyes and imagine yourself transforming into a robot. Feel the power in your legs as they become metallic, hydraulic power houses, capable of relentless powerful pedalling. Feel the power flowing through you. Let each breath in and out take you deeper into the cool, emotionless, detached mindset of a robot.

• Keep this internal visualization locked in, ever present in the back of your mind even as you walk about and prepare for your ride or race. Perhaps in the back of your mind start to 'program' in two or three core programs or goals for the ride like "stay in front group" or "conserve energy for sprint"

2. **During the Ride:**

• When you feel yourself slipping into doubt or distraction, repeat a cue word or phrase like "robot mode" or "mechanical precision." Let out a big long breath and let yourself slip into that cool, emotionless and slightly detached mindset.

• Visualize becoming one with your bike. Metal arms and legs fusing into handlebars and pedals creating one machine. Imaging readouts showing that the system is running perfectly and there is plenty of power in the system.

- Keep saying the core programs you set before the ride in your head or maybe you want to take it even further and chose some targets to follow and imagine that The Robot's job is to stick with those cyclists no matter what. Have fun! Create some crosshairs in your vision and get them locked onto the riders you want to stick with or bridge a gap to.

3. **Post-Ride Reflection:**

- After the ride, reflect on how it felt to embody the robot mindset. Did it help you stay focused or enter flow? Use these insights to refine your visualization practice.

Time Distortion: A Robotic Perception of Time

Robots don't perceive time like humans—they operate with efficiency, no matter the duration of the task. You can use this idea to manipulate your perception of time during challenging efforts. Spend time in The Robot during your ride to help the time pass, drift in and out of it as you want to.

Speeding Up Time During Discomfort

- Imagine your robotic mind compressing time during long, painful efforts (like a time trial). Visualize the miles flying by as if you're fast-forwarding through the experience.

Slowing Time During a Sprint

- During a sprint, visualize your robotic sensors slowing everything around you. Picture other riders moving in slow motion while you remain at full speed, allowing you to make strategic decisions with ease.

Conclusion: Embrace Your Inner Robot

The robot cyclist visualization isn't about stripping away the joy or passion of cycling—it's about giving yourself a mental tool to override distractions, quiet self-doubt, and achieve peak performance. By embodying the calm, precise mindset of a machine, you can access flow states, manage emotional challenges, and push past mental barriers. Practice this visualization regularly, combine it with anchoring techniques, and watch as your cycling performance reaches a new level of focus and resilience. Let's flip the switch and ride like machines!

11 From Relaxed to Alert

Self-hypnosis is often associated with a relaxed state—sitting or lying quietly, eyes closed, fully focused on your inner world. While this is a fantastic starting point, the true power of self-hypnosis emerges when you can take that same focused mental state and apply it in the middle of action—whether that's walking, riding your bike, or navigating the mental and physical challenges of a tough climb or sprint.

This chapter will guide you through the process of transitioning from relaxed hypnosis to alert hypnosis, teaching you how to maintain the benefits of a hypnotic state even as you move and engage with the world around you. By developing a "hypnotic base," much like building aerobic fitness in cycling, you'll create the mental resilience and focus needed to access alert hypnosis during your rides, whether it's for managing pain, finding flow, or enhancing focus.

Building Your Hypnotic Base: Start with Relaxed Hypnosis

Just as cyclists start their training with base miles to build endurance, transitioning to alert hypnosis begins with mastering relaxed hypnosis. The more comfortable and experienced you become with relaxed hypnosis, the easier it will be to maintain the hypnotic state while in motion.

Strengthening Your Foundation

1. **Start with Muscle Relaxation**

• Progressive Muscle Relaxation (PMR) is one of the best ways to familiarize yourself with the hypnotic state. By systematically tensing and releasing each muscle group, you build the ability to focus your attention inward and quiet your mind. Practice PMR regularly until you can easily enter a calm, focused state.

2. **Practice Visualization in Relaxed Hypnosis**

• While in a relaxed state, practice vivid visualizations (as taught in earlier chapters). For example, picture yourself riding smoothly, staying calm, or conquering a challenging climb. The goal is to build confidence in accessing and maintaining this focused mental state.

3. **Anchor Your Hypnotic State**

- Develop an anchor—a physical action, word, or gesture—that you associate with entering hypnosis. For example, pressing your thumb and forefinger together while in a relaxed hypnotic state can act as a trigger to help you access hypnosis later, even in active situations.

Transitioning to Alert Hypnosis: Keeping the Focus While Moving

Once you're confident in your ability to enter a hypnotic state while relaxed, it's time to transition to alert hypnosis. This involves maintaining a focused, hypnotic mindset even as you engage in physical activities.

Step 1: Eye Fixation with Eyes Open

Eye fixation is a bridge between relaxed and alert hypnosis. While in relaxed hypnosis, your eyes are typically closed to limit distractions. In this step, you'll practice maintaining the hypnotic state with your eyes open.

How to Practice:

1. **Find a Fixed Point:** Choose a point to focus on—a spot on the wall, or a specific object in your environment. A great one and this can be used pretty much anywhere is to just lay your hand on your lap and chose a spot on your hand or perhaps a particular nail.

2. **Enter Relaxation:** Begin with a few deep breaths and allow your focus to soften as you fixate on the point. Notice the shift in your attention as your mind becomes calm and centered.

3. **Maintain the Shift:** Instead of closing your eyes as you did in previous practice, keep your eyes open while holding onto that calm, focused state.

4. **Deep Breathing:** Use slow, rhythmic breathing to help maintain the hypnotic state with your eyes open. Breathe in for four counts, hold for four, and exhale for six.

Goal: Practice holding this state for longer periods, even as your awareness of your surroundings increases.

Step 2: Alert Hypnosis in Motion

Once you can maintain a hypnotic state with eyes open, the next step is to introduce movement. This helps you practice staying focused while engaging in light, repetitive activities.

How to Practice:

1. **Start with Walking:**

    • Enter a relaxed hypnotic state using your preferred induction technique.

    • Once in hypnosis, begin walking slowly, focusing on the rhythm of your steps. Imagine each step grounding your focus deeper into the present moment.

    • Use affirmations like, "I am calm and focused with every step," or "Each step deepens my concentration."

2. **Add Complexity Gradually:**

    • Practice alert hypnosis during other activities, such as stretching, household chores, or walking through a park. The goal is to maintain your focus even as you engage in more complex movements.

Using Alert Hypnosis on the Bike

THE CYCLIST'S MIND

Cycling is the perfect activity for practicing alert hypnosis, especially during turbo sessions. The repetitive motion of pedaling and the controlled environment make it easier to maintain focus and deepen your practice.

Step 1: Turbo Sessions

Turbo trainers are excellent for practicing alert hypnosis because they eliminate external distractions like traffic or terrain, allowing you to focus entirely on your mental state.

How to Practice on the Turbo Trainer:

1. **Set the Scene:**

• Begin your turbo session as you would a relaxed hypnosis session. Use eye fixation to enter a calm, focused state before you start pedalling.

2. **Focus on Rhythm:**

• Focus on your breathing and let each deep exhale take your attending back into hypnosis, or if you come out of hypnosis for a while, take two quick breaths and then let the third long exhale take you back in as you refocus on the spot used for eye fixation. These quick two breaths and then one long one out are a great way of delving back into hypnosis very quickly before an interval starts and the more often you do this the quicker you will be able to shift back into this state out on the road too.

•	Visualize your legs as smooth, efficient pistons, moving with mechanical precision.

3.	**Expand Awareness:**

•	Gradually bring your attention to the sensations of riding—the feel of the pedals, the sound of the chain, the rhythm of your breath. Practice staying in the hypnotic state even as you become more aware of your surroundings.

Step 2: Road Rides

Once you've practiced alert hypnosis on the turbo, it's time to take it out on the road. Start with low-stress rides and gradually incorporate alert hypnosis into more challenging scenarios.

How to Use Alert Hypnosis While Riding:

1.	**Enter Hypnosis Before the Ride:**

•	Use a quick induction technique before heading out, such as eye fixation or breathing focus.

2. **Engage During the Ride:**

- Practice staying in the hypnotic state by focusing on repetitive sensations—your pedalling cadence, the sound of your tires, or the rhythm of your breath.

- Use affirmations like, "I am in control of my mind and body," or "Each mile strengthens my focus."

3. **Handle Challenges:**

- During tough climbs, sprints, or moments of discomfort, anchor your hypnotic state using a trigger, such as gripping the handlebars or repeating a specific word like "focus" or "flow."

4. **Visualizations:**

- This is now where you can use internal visualizations such as the Pain Dial or The Robot to manage discomfort, mindset or access flow.

Troubleshooting Common Challenges

Moving from relaxed to alert hypnosis can feel challenging at first. Here are some common issues and how to address them:

1. **Losing Focus Mid-Activity:**

• If you find your mind wandering, use the two quick breaths and then one long exhale to re-center yourself.

2. **Difficulty Entering Hypnosis on the Bike:**

• Start with shorter rides or low-intensity efforts until you feel more confident maintaining the hypnotic state.

3. **Overthinking the Process:**

• Remember, hypnosis is a natural state. Trust the process and focus on small improvements rather than perfection.

Conclusion: Taking Self-Hypnosis to the Next Level

Moving from relaxed hypnosis to alert hypnosis opens up a world of possibilities for applying mental training to your cycling performance. By practicing the transition gradually—first with relaxed techniques, then with eye fixation, walking, and turbo sessions—you'll build the mental strength and focus needed to access hypnosis even in the heat of a tough ride.

THE CYCLIST'S MIND

With practice, alert hypnosis will become a natural part of your mental toolkit, helping you manage pain, stay focused, and perform at your peak.

THE CYCLIST'S MIND

12 ALTERED STATES & FLOW

Cycling is more than just a physical activity; it's a state of mind. From the hypnotic rhythm of pedalling to the exhilaration of a perfect descent, there are moments on the bike when everything clicks. Time seems to warp, your movements feel effortless, and your mind is completely absorbed in the ride. This elusive experience is often referred to as "flow"—a state of optimal performance where you're fully immersed in the moment.

But flow doesn't just happen by chance. With self-hypnosis, you can train your mind to shift into altered states of consciousness, harness the power of flow on demand, and even manipulate your perception of time to enhance your performance. Additionally, by using techniques like anchoring, you can create mental triggers that allow you to access confidence, focus, or power whenever you need it.

In this chapter, we'll explore how self-hypnosis can help you shift perceptions and states, understand the science of flow, harness time distortion, and learn to set anchors for peak performance.

Shifting Perceptions and States with Self-Hypnosis

At its core, self-hypnosis is about creating a deliberate shift in your mental and emotional state. Whether you need to calm pre-race nerves, push through pain, or access a burst of power for a sprint, self-hypnosis allows you to take control of your inner world.

The Power of Altered States

An altered state of consciousness is simply a mental state that feels different from your usual waking state. These states aren't as mysterious as they sound—you've likely experienced them naturally. Ever gotten so absorbed in a task that you lost track of time? Or found yourself daydreaming while cycling? These are examples of altered states.

Through self-hypnosis, you can enter these states intentionally, unlocking the subconscious mind to:

• Reframe pain and discomfort as manageable or even empowering.

• Heighten focus and clarity during critical moments.

• Boost creativity for problem-solving during a ride.

•	Enhance emotional resilience by shifting into a calm or confident mindset.

The Role of Self-Hypnosis

Self-hypnosis acts as a bridge between your conscious and subconscious mind, allowing you to guide your mental state with intention. By practicing self-hypnosis, you can:

•	Quiet distractions and tune into your body's sensations and rhythm.

•	Access the right mental state for each cycling challenge, whether it's grit for a climb or relaxation during recovery.

•	Train your brain to enter altered states more easily, building a foundation for achieving flow and mastering time perception.

Flow: The Zone Where Everything Clicks

Flow is the ultimate altered state for athletes. It's that magical moment when you're completely absorbed in the ride, and everything feels effortless. Your movements are precise, your mind is calm, and you're performing at your peak.

The Science of Flow

Flow was first described by psychologist Mihaly Csikszentmihalyi, who found that people experience their highest levels of performance and satisfaction when in this state. Here's what happens during flow:

- Intense Focus: Your attention narrows to the task at hand, eliminating distractions.

- Effortless Action: Your body and mind work in perfect harmony, with movements feeling automatic and smooth.

- Altered Time Perception: Time may feel like it's speeding up or slowing down.

- Increased Creativity: Your brain generates solutions and strategies effortlessly.

- Reduced Self-Consciousness: Doubts and fears fade away, leaving you fully immersed in the experience.

For cyclists, flow might occur during a fast descent, a perfectly executed sprint, or a long ride where every pedal stroke feels natural.

Self-Hypnosis and Flow

Self-hypnosis is an ideal tool for accessing flow because it trains your mind to focus, quiet distractions, and enter a state of heightened awareness. By visualizing flow states during hypnosis, you can prepare your brain to recognize and slip into them more easily during your rides.

Time Distortion: Bending the Clock to Your Advantage

Time distortion is a fascinating phenomenon where your perception of time speeds up or slows down, allowing you to manipulate how you experience specific moments. This altered perception of time is often linked to altered states like flow or hypnosis.

How Time Distortion Works

Your brain processes time based on attention and emotional engagement. When you're fully absorbed in an activity, time can feel like it's flying by. Conversely, when you focus intently on every detail, time seems to stretch out. This may sound crazy initially but just think about how time can seem to fly by when you are doing something pleasurable yet drags when doing some mundane chore. How we experience time can be controlled. This technique is commonly taught to women in labour to increase the experience of time between contractions and also to speed up the experience of time during contractions.

Using Time Distortion for Cycling

1. Speeding Up Discomfort: During long periods of sustained effort, such as a time trial, you can use self-hypnosis to make time feel like it's passing more quickly. By narrowing your focus to rhythmic breathing or pedalling cadence, you shift attention away from the clock and discomfort. Even if you are uncomfortable, try to take immense pleasure in what you are doing, remember how time passes more quickly when doing something you are enjoying? Use that as well to help time flow more quickly.

2. Slowing Down for Precision: In high-speed moments, such as a sprint or navigating a chaotic race, you can slow your perception of time to enhance decision-making. By focusing intently on the moment, you create the sensation of having more time to react while maintaining full speed.

These are things that can take practice and when it comes to real-life settings after doing these techniques off the bike, you may not even notice that much of a difference in what you are experiencing. But, especially when slowing time down, you are priming your nervous system to operate at a higher speed and increase things like reaction time and ability to make decisions more quickly.

Self-Hypnosis for Time Distortion

1. To Speed Up Time:

• During hypnosis, visualize yourself riding effortlessly through a time trial. Imagine the minutes flying by as you remain steady and strong.

• While riding, sync your focus to your pedalling cadence, imagining that each stroke brings you closer to the finish in no time at all.

2. To Slow Down Time:

• Before a sprint, visualize yourself in a heightened state of awareness. See the road and competitors in slow motion while you move and think at normal speed giving you time to make precise decisions.

• During the sprint, focus on each movement—shifting gears, gripping the handlebars, and accelerating—feeling as though time slows around you while you remain fast and powerful.

Anchoring: Creating Mental Triggers for Peak Performance

Anchoring is a powerful technique used in hypnosis to create mental triggers that can shift your state instantly. Think of it as pressing a mental "button" that activates a specific feeling, like confidence, focus, or power. For cyclists, anchoring can be invaluable in high-pressure situations, like race starts or final sprints.

What is Anchoring?

Anchoring is based on the principle of association. Just as a certain song can instantly evoke a memory or emotion, you can train your mind to associate a specific physical or verbal cue with a desired state. Once the anchor is established, you can use it to access that state whenever you need it. Once you become aware of what anchors you will likely notice athletes using them on TV. Notice anyone touching thumb and forefinger together which is a common place to put anchors or pressing on their earlobe. If you see someone doing that then they are more than likely using an anchor to access a certain resource or state of mind.

Examples of Anchors for Cyclists

- Confidence Anchor: Squeezing the handlebars while repeating a phrase like "I am unstoppable" to activate confidence before a race.

- Power Anchor: Clenching your fists and saying "Full power" to unleash maximum effort during a sprint.

- Calm Anchor: Touching your thumb and forefinger together while saying "I am calm and composed" to manage pre-race nerves.

Using Self-Hypnosis to Access Flow, Time Distortion, and Anchors

Now that you understand flow, time distortion, and anchoring, let's explore how to use self-hypnosis to unlock these powerful tools.

Accessing Flow with Self-Hypnosis

Ok so up until now flow and self-hypnosis have been two separate concepts and I have been telling you that self-hypnosis can be a tool to help get into flow. Which is correct. However now we are further into our journey together, I want you to now put the thought aside that they are two separate 'states' and see that self-hypnosis IS flow. Once you are able to access alert hypnosis, just feeling that shift in your mindset by following the processes I have shown you, you can access flow at any time.

What you experience internally when accessing self-hypnosis is essentially the same as flow. So, by adopting this shift in thinking of them as being two separate concepts, instead of flow being something that occasionally happens with no actual control over when, you now have the ability to get into flow at will and this is something which is immensely powerful and cannot be underestimated.

Setting Anchors with Self-Hypnosis

1. Choose a Desired State: Decide what you want the anchor to trigger—confidence, focus, power, or calmness.

2. Select a Cue: Pick a physical or verbal cue, such as gripping the handlebars, clenching your fists, or saying a specific word.

3. Enter a Hypnotic State: Use self-hypnosis to calm your mind and focus on your goal.

4. Pair the Cue with the State: While in a deeply focused state, imagine yourself feeling the desired emotion (e.g.,

confidence or power). As you do, activate your chosen cue—for example, grip the handlebars and say "I am unstoppable."

5. Repeat and Reinforce: Practice this pairing several times during the session. Over time, the association between the cue and the state will strengthen.

6. Test the Anchor: During a ride, activate the anchor by using your cue. Notice how your mind and body respond.

This is a technique which you may need to pay attention to notice a difference immediately. Some people notice huge effects immediately, some might notice a slight change and need to build on it more through repeating the process and strengthening the anchor.

Power During a Sprint

1. Visualize yourself launching a powerful sprint, feeling explosive energy surging through your legs.

2. Clench your fists and say, "Full power," while imagining yourself accelerating past your competitors with ease. Again, really utilise emotions and feelings to create a really powerful experience.

3.   Practice pairing this physical and verbal cue during self-hypnosis and on the turbo trainer until it becomes automatic.

4.   During a sprint in real life, clench your fists (or grip the handlebars) and repeat "Full power" to activate the anchored feeling of strength and speed.

Calmness in Pre-Race Nerves

1.   Use self-hypnosis to imagine yourself at the start line of a big event. Picture the scene in vivid detail—hear the chatter of other cyclists, feel the cool morning air, and see the course stretching ahead.

2.   Pair the visualization with a calming anchor, such as pressing your thumb and forefinger together while repeating, "I am calm and composed."

3.   Reinforce this anchor during multiple sessions, associating it with a deep sense of inner calm.

4.   On race day, use the anchor as you line up, activating that same calm confidence.

Endurance During a Climb

1. Visualize yourself climbing a long, relentless hill. Imagine every pedal stroke feeling strong and steady, with your breathing in rhythm.

2. Use a physical anchor, such as pressing your handlebars with your palms, while repeating, "Every pedal stroke makes me stronger."

3. Practice this pairing during self-hypnosis and on actual climbs.

4. When tackling a tough ascent, press into the bars and repeat your affirmation to activate the anchored endurance.

Conclusion: Mastering Altered States for Peak Performance

Cycling is as much a mental game as a physical one, and mastering altered states can transform your performance. By using self-hypnosis, you can intentionally shift your perception of pain, time, and effort, helping you achieve feats that might have previously felt impossible.

With flow, you can immerse yourself fully in the ride, performing at your peak without overthinking. With time distortion, you can bend your perception of time to endure discomfort more easily or react with lightning precision. And with anchoring, you can create powerful mental triggers that give you confidence, power, and focus whenever you need them.

These tools aren't just theoretical—they're practical strategies you can integrate into your rides, races, and training sessions. Like all aspects of self-hypnosis, the key is practice and repetition. The more you use these techniques, the more naturally they'll come to you, and the stronger your mental edge will become.

Now, it's time to take what you've learned and apply it. As you ride, experiment with anchoring, practice entering flow, and see how time distortion can shift your experience. With these techniques in your mental toolbox, the road ahead is limitless.

13 MENTAL TOUGHNESS

Mental toughness is often misunderstood. It's not about pretending to be invincible, suppressing emotions, or adopting an outdated "tough guy/girl" attitude. In fact, true mental toughness is about resilience, adaptability, and what some experts call "bouncebackability"—the ability to recover and grow stronger after setbacks. It's about staying composed under pressure, persisting when the going gets tough, and remaining focused on your goals even in the face of adversity.

For cyclists, mental toughness is as critical as physical endurance. Whether you're struggling through a relentless climb, recovering from a crash, or simply battling the voice in your head telling you to quit, it's mental toughness that keeps you moving forward.

The 4 Cs of Mental Toughness

The concept of mental toughness has been broken down into four key components, known as the 4 Cs: Control, Commitment,

Challenge, and Confidence. Together, these elements form the foundation of mental resilience and high performance.

1. Control

Control is your ability to stay composed and regulate your emotions, even in challenging situations. It's about feeling that you have some agency over what's happening, rather than being overwhelmed by circumstances. In cycling, control might mean staying calm during a chaotic race start or maintaining focus when your ride doesn't go as planned.

2. Commitment

Commitment is your ability to set goals and stick to them, no matter the obstacles. It's the determination to follow through on your plans, even when the motivation wanes or the conditions become difficult. For cyclists, this could mean sticking to your training schedule on rainy days or pushing through the final kilometers of a gruelling ride.

3. Challenge

Challenge is your willingness to view obstacles as opportunities for growth rather than threats. It's about embracing difficulties as a chance to learn and improve, rather than shying away from them. In cycling, this mindset helps you see every tough climb or intense interval as a stepping stone toward becoming a stronger rider.

4. Confidence

Confidence is the belief in your ability to succeed. It's not arrogance; it's the quiet, steady belief that you have what it takes to achieve your goals. Confidence allows you to face challenges with optimism and trust in your preparation. For cyclists, it's the difference between starting a race with self-doubt and starting with self-assurance.

How Self-Hypnosis Builds Mental Toughness

By now, you're probably already seeing how self-hypnosis is the perfect tool for building mental toughness. Each of the 4 Cs involves your mindset, emotions, and subconscious beliefs—all areas where self-hypnosis excels. Here's how:

1. Control: Hypnosis helps you regulate your emotions by calming your nervous system and reframing stressful

situations. When you practice self-hypnosis, you're training your mind to stay composed under pressure.

2.	Commitment: Through visualization and affirmations, self-hypnosis reinforces your goals and strengthens your resolve to stick to them, even when the going gets tough.

3.	Challenge: Hypnosis helps you reframe challenges as opportunities for growth. By visualizing yourself succeeding in difficult situations, you train your brain to approach obstacles with curiosity and determination.

4.	Confidence: Self-hypnosis builds confidence by planting positive suggestions in your subconscious mind. Over time, these affirmations replace self-doubt with a steady belief in your abilities.

Now, let's take a deeper dive into how you can use self-hypnosis to strengthen each of the 4 Cs. In the following sections, you'll find hypnosis suggestions and visualization exercises tailored to each aspect of mental toughness.

Control: Staying Composed Under Pressure

When you feel in control, challenges become manageable. The key is learning how to stay calm and centered, no matter the situation.

Hypnosis Suggestions for Control

- "With every breath, I feel calmer and more composed."

- "I remain steady and focused, no matter what happens around me."

- "In every situation, I choose calm over chaos."

Visualization for Control

1. Imagine a Stressful Situation: Picture yourself at the start of a race, surrounded by the buzz of nervous energy. Instead of feeling overwhelmed, visualize yourself breathing deeply and staying calm.

2. Focus on Your Breath: See yourself using deep, rhythmic breathing to stay grounded. With each breath, you feel more composed.

3. See the Outcome: Imagine navigating the situation with poise and finishing strong, feeling proud of how you stayed in control.

Commitment: Sticking to Your Goals

Commitment is about showing up, even when it's hard. Self-hypnosis can reinforce your determination and help you push through when motivation falters.

Hypnosis Suggestions for Commitment

- "Every day, I am becoming more committed to my goals."

- "The more I stick to my plans, the stronger and more capable I become."

- "Every ride I complete brings me closer to my dreams."

Visualization for Commitment

1. Picture a Goal: Visualize a specific goal, like completing a 100-mile ride or sticking to your training plan for a month.

2. See the Obstacles: Imagine the challenges you might face—bad weather, fatigue, or self-doubt.

3.   Overcome Each One: Visualize yourself overcoming each obstacle with determination. See yourself lacing up your shoes in the rain, pushing through fatigue, or silencing self-doubt with positive self-talk.

4.   Feel the Success: End by imagining the pride and satisfaction of achieving your goal, knowing you stayed committed.

Challenge: Embracing Growth Opportunities

Challenges are inevitable, but how you view them makes all the difference. Self-hypnosis helps you see difficulties as opportunities to grow stronger.

Hypnosis Suggestions for Challenge

- "Every challenge I face helps me grow stronger and wiser."
- "I welcome obstacles as opportunities to improve."
- "The tougher the challenge, the greater my growth."

Visualization for Challenge

1. Picture a Tough Climb: Imagine yourself on a steep hill that feels impossible.

2. Reframe the Challenge: Instead of dreading it, visualize it as an exciting opportunity to prove your strength.

3. Feel the Effort: Picture yourself pedaling steadily, feeling the burn in your legs as a sign of progress.

4. Celebrate the Growth: See yourself reaching the top, stronger and more confident than before.

Confidence: Believing in Yourself

Confidence is the cornerstone of mental toughness. With self-hypnosis, you can replace self-doubt with a steady belief in your abilities.

Hypnosis Suggestions for Confidence

- "Every day, I am becoming more confident in my abilities."

- "Every ride I complete builds my strength and self-belief."

- "When I ride, I feel calm, capable, and unstoppable."

Visualization for Confidence

1. Picture a Moment of Success: Visualize a time when you felt confident and strong, whether it was a great training ride or a race victory.

2. Recreate the Feeling: Imagine the sights, sounds, and emotions of that moment. Feel the pride, strength, and joy in your body.

3. Project it Forward: Visualize yourself carrying that same confidence into your next ride or race, performing with poise and self-assurance.

Conclusion: Building Mental Toughness One Step at a Time

Mental toughness isn't something you're born with—it's something you build, one step at a time. By focusing on the 4 Cs—Control, Commitment, Challenge, and Confidence—you can develop the resilience, determination, and self-belief needed to tackle any challenge, on or off the bike.

Self-hypnosis is your secret weapon in this journey. With each session, you're strengthening your mind, rewiring your subconscious, and unlocking a new level of mental strength.

Practice the techniques and suggestions in this chapter regularly, and watch as your mental toughness transforms—not just in cycling, but in every area of your life. Let's keep riding toward greater resilience and strength!

14 SETBACKS & 'FAILURES'

Setbacks and failures are an inevitable part of cycling—and life. No matter how much you prepare, train, or visualize success, there will always be moments that don't go to plan. Maybe it's a flat tire during a race, an injury that takes you out of training, or a race where your performance doesn't meet your expectations. But here's the truth: failure is not the end—it's feedback.

Every setback is an opportunity to learn, grow, and come back stronger. The key is how you choose to respond. With the right mindset and tools, like self-hypnosis, you can transform every stumble into a stepping stone toward progress.

Reframing Failure: Feedback, Not Defeat

The idea that failure is the opposite of success is a myth. In reality, failure is an essential part of success. Every athlete, from weekend warriors to world champions, has faced moments of disappointment. What sets successful people apart is their ability to see setbacks as valuable feedback.

Why Setbacks Are Opportunities:

1. Clarity: A setback reveals areas for growth. For example, if you struggled on a climb, it might highlight areas to focus on, like strength or pacing.

2. Resilience: Each challenge you overcome makes you mentally tougher, preparing you for future obstacles.

3. Perspective: Failure teaches humility and reminds us that the journey is just as important as the destination.

Think of setbacks as your most honest coach. They don't sugarcoat or flatter; they show you exactly where you stand and where you can improve. Embracing this mindset turns every so-called failure into a chance to learn and adapt.

How Self-Hypnosis Helps You Bounce Back

When setbacks strike, it's easy to let frustration, self-doubt, or negativity take over. This is where self-hypnosis becomes a game-changer. By accessing your subconscious mind, self-hypnosis helps you reframe setbacks, build resilience, and regain confidence.

Key Benefits of Self-Hypnosis for Setbacks:

1. Reframing Experiences: Hypnosis allows you to reframe failure as growth. Instead of thinking, "I'm not good enough," you can shift to, "I'm learning what I need to improve."

2. Calming Emotional Reactions: Setbacks often trigger frustration, anger, or self-doubt. Hypnosis helps you process these emotions calmly and constructively.

3. Rebuilding Confidence: By reinforcing affirmations and visualizing future success, self-hypnosis restores your belief in your abilities.

4. Creating a Forward-Focused Mindset: Rather than dwelling on the past, hypnosis helps you focus on the lessons learned and the steps ahead.

Practical Example:
Imagine finishing a race far behind your personal goal. With self-hypnosis, you can revisit the race in a relaxed state, reframe it as a learning experience, and visualize yourself executing a smarter strategy next time.

No Setback Is Too Big: The Power of Growth Mindset

A growth mindset—the belief that abilities can be developed through effort and learning—is essential for transforming setbacks into opportunities. Self-hypnosis is a powerful tool for cultivating this mindset. It helps you replace fixed, limiting beliefs (e.g., "I'll never be good at climbing") with empowering ones (e.g., "With practice, I get stronger on every climb").

Hypnosis Suggestions for a Growth Mindset:

- "Every challenge I face helps me grow stronger and smarter."
- "I embrace setbacks as opportunities to improve."
- "Each time I get back on the bike, I become more resilient."

Common Setbacks and Hypnotic Strategies to Overcome Them

Let's explore some common challenges cyclists face and how you can use self-hypnosis to navigate them with confidence and resilience.

1. Poor Race Performance

Visualization: Picture yourself reviewing the race calmly, identifying what went well and where you can improve. See yourself executing those improvements in the next event. Suggestions:

- "Every race, no matter the outcome, teaches me how to be a better cyclist."

- "I am becoming a smarter, stronger rider with every competition."

- "I focus on the lessons, not the losses."

2. Injury and Recovery

Visualization: Imagine your body healing efficiently and growing stronger with every day of rest and rehabilitation. Picture yourself returning to the bike with renewed focus and strength. Suggestions:

- "My body is healing, and I grow stronger with every day."

- "This time of recovery is building my resilience."

- "I will come back smarter, stronger, and more determined."

3. Missed Training Goals

Visualization: Picture yourself adjusting your training plan with flexibility and focus, making steady progress toward your goals despite the setback.

Suggestions:

- "Every adjustment I make improves my long-term progress."
- "I am adaptable and committed to my goals."
- "Missed sessions are opportunities to refine my approach."

4. Fear of Failure

Visualization: Imagine yourself calmly preparing for a race or challenging ride, focusing on your strengths and strategies rather than the fear of failure.

Suggestions:

- "I trust my preparation and embrace the challenge."
- "Every ride is an opportunity to grow, not a test to fear."

- "I approach each challenge with confidence and curiosity."

5. Struggling on a Tough Climb

Visualization: Picture yourself tackling a climb with steady determination, breaking it into manageable sections and celebrating small victories along the way.

Suggestions:

- "Each pedal stroke brings me closer to the top."
- "I am strong and capable, no matter the challenge."
- "Every climb I face makes me a better cyclist."

6. Group Ride Struggles

Visualization: Imagine yourself staying composed and confident in a group setting, holding your line and making smart decisions.

Suggestions:

- "I ride my own race and trust my abilities."
- "I stay calm and focused, no matter the pace."
- "Each group ride is an opportunity to build my confidence."

Conclusion: Turning Setbacks Into Stepping Stones

Setbacks are not roadblocks; they're stepping stones on the path to growth. By reframing failure as feedback, embracing a growth mindset, and using self-hypnosis to process and overcome challenges, you'll not only bounce back—you'll come back stronger.

The journey of cycling, like life, is filled with highs and lows. The key is not to avoid the lows but to use them to propel you higher. With the tools in this chapter, you're equipped to face any setback with resilience, focus, and confidence. Let's keep pedalling forward, turning every challenge into an opportunity for growth!

15 RECOVERY

Recovery is as crucial to a cyclist's success as training itself. It's during recovery that your body repairs muscles, replenishes energy stores, and builds the adaptations that make you stronger. However, recovery isn't just a physical process—it's deeply influenced by your mental state. Stress, poor sleep, and negative emotions can hinder your body's ability to recover effectively. This is where self-hypnosis and visualization come into play.

By engaging your mind, you can promote deeper relaxation, lower stress hormones like cortisol, and create a mental environment that supports optimal recovery. Combined with scientific insights into immunity, hormones, and the mind-body connection, this chapter will show you how to supercharge your recovery with the power of your mind.

The Science of Recovery: The Role of the Mind and Body

Cortisol and Stress

Cortisol, often referred to as the "stress hormone," plays a key role in recovery. While it's essential in small doses to manage energy and inflammation, chronically high cortisol levels—often caused by stress—can impair your body's ability to repair itself. Elevated cortisol can:

- Suppress immune function, making you more susceptible to illness.

- Inhibit muscle repair and adaptation.

- Disrupt sleep, which is critical for recovery.

The Immune System and Recovery

Cycling, especially at high intensities, temporarily suppresses the immune system. This is why athletes are more prone to illness after hard training or races. Visualization and relaxation techniques can support immune health by:

- Reducing stress hormones that suppress immunity.

- Encouraging deeper, restorative sleep.

- Creating a mental state that promotes balance in the body.

Visualization as a Recovery Tool

Scientific studies have shown that visualization can have a direct impact on physical processes. By imagining healing and restoration, you can:

- Enhance parasympathetic nervous system activity (the "rest and digest" system).

- Reduce inflammation and perceived fatigue.

- Encourage a sense of calm and well-being, which supports overall recovery.

Healing Visualizations for Recovery

Visualization is a versatile tool for enhancing recovery. By focusing your mind on specific images and sensations, you can mentally guide your body toward relaxation, repair, and rejuvenation. The following visualizations are designed to target key aspects of recovery, from muscle repair to stress reduction.

1. Healing White Light Visualization

The healing white light visualization is a powerful technique for promoting a sense of total-body recovery. It encourages your mind to focus on healing and balance, creating a mental state conducive to physical repair.

Steps:

1. Enter Relaxation: Begin by using a progressive muscle relaxation induction or deep breathing to calm your body and mind.

2. Visualize the Light: Imagine a warm, white light entering your body through the top of your head. Use all your senses to make it as powerful as possible. Hear it hum as you become aware of its immense healing power. This light is filled with healing energy, capable of repairing and restoring every cell in your body.

3. Guide the Light: Slowly move the light through your body, starting at your head and moving down to your toes. As it flows, picture the light releasing tension, soothing soreness, and repairing damaged muscles.

4. Feel the Effects: Imagine the light leaving a trail of relaxation and renewal in its wake. Visualize your cells being replenished and your immune system strengthening.

5. Finish with Affirmations: Repeat phrases like:

- "This light restores my body and fills me with energy."

- "Every moment of rest helps me grow stronger."

2. Passive Muscle Relaxation with Healing Visualization

This technique combines muscle relaxation with a focused visualization of healing entering the muscles. It's ideal for post-ride recovery when your muscles feel tight or fatigued.

Steps:

1. Relax the Body: Sit or lie down comfortably and take several deep breaths. Imagine each breath bringing calm and relaxation into your body.

2. Focus on One Muscle Group at a Time: Start with your feet and work your way up to your head. With each muscle group:

- Inhale and imagine the area being filled with a soothing, healing sensation (like a warm liquid or a soft glow).

- Exhale and visualize any tension or soreness leaving your body as dark smoke or a fading shadow.

3. Visualize the Healing Process: Picture your muscles absorbing the healing energy, repairing microtears, and flushing out waste products like lactic acid.

4. Feel Gratitude: As you work through each muscle group, silently thank your body for its strength and effort during your ride.

5. Affirm Your Recovery: Use affirmations such as:

• "With every breath, my muscles grow stronger and more resilient."

• "Healing energy flows through me, repairing and restoring my body."

3. Cellular Restoration Visualization

This technique focuses on healing at the cellular level, reinforcing the idea that your body is working hard to repair and strengthen itself after every ride.

Steps:

1. Set the Scene: Imagine yourself shrinking down to the size of a single cell and entering your own body.

2. Visualize Cellular Activity: Picture your cells as tiny workers, actively repairing tissue, replenishing glycogen stores, and rebuilding muscle fibers. See them working efficiently and effectively.

3. Focus on Specific Areas: Direct your attention to areas of the body that feel sore or fatigued. Imagine the cells in those areas working even harder, clearing out waste products and delivering fresh nutrients.

4. Enhance the Visualization: Add details such as the sound of tiny tools repairing muscle fibres or the glow of energy being delivered to your cells.

5. Affirm Your Progress: Repeat affirmations like:

- "Every cell in my body is working in perfect harmony to repair and restore."

- "My body is a powerful machine, designed to heal and grow stronger."

4. Nature-Based Visualization for Recovery

This visualization uses imagery from nature to create a sense of deep calm and renewal.

Steps:

1. Choose a Natural Setting: Imagine yourself in a peaceful, restorative place in nature, such as a forest, a mountain meadow, or by a tranquil stream.

2. Connect with Nature's Healing Energy: Picture the air around you filled with energy that promotes healing. As you breathe in, imagine this energy entering your body and spreading through your muscles and cells.

3. Use Symbolism: Visualize your body as a tree, with strong roots drawing in nourishment from the earth. As the nutrients flow upward, they repair and strengthen every part of you.

4. Focus on Renewal: Imagine the gentle breeze or flowing water washing away any tension, fatigue, or soreness.

5. Reinforce with Affirmations: Use statements such as:

- "I am connected to the earth, and its energy restores me."

- "Nature's healing power renews my body and mind."

The Importance of Consistency in Recovery Practices

Just as physical training requires regular effort, recovery practices like hypnosis and visualization yield the best results when practiced consistently. Incorporate these visualizations into your post-ride routine or during rest days to maximize their impact.

Key Benefits of Consistent Practice:

- Improved Sleep Quality: Visualization promotes relaxation, helping you fall asleep faster and stay asleep longer.

- Reduced Stress: Lower cortisol levels mean better recovery and reduced risk of overtraining.

- Enhanced Immune Function: Regular relaxation and visualization strengthen your body's natural defences, keeping you healthy and ready to ride.

Conclusion: Recovery as a Mental and Physical Practice

Recovery isn't just about lying on the couch—it's an active process that requires the engagement of both your body and mind. By using self-hypnosis and visualization techniques, you can create a mental environment that supports your body's natural healing processes. Whether you're visualizing a healing light, engaging in passive muscle relaxation, or connecting with nature's energy, these tools empower you to recover smarter and faster.

The road to peak performance isn't just about how hard you can push—it's also about how well you can recover. With these techniques, you'll be ready to take on your next ride stronger, healthier, and more focused than ever. Let's keep pedalling forward—renewed, resilient, and ready for the next challenge.

16 TROUBLESHOOTING SELF HYPNOSIS

Self-hypnosis is a transformative tool, but like any skill, it comes with its own set of challenges. From wandering thoughts to doubts about whether it's working, it's common to encounter roadblocks along the way. The key is to treat these obstacles as opportunities for growth rather than reasons to give up. Every difficulty offers valuable insight into your practice, helping you refine your approach and deepen your understanding.

This chapter will address common challenges in self-hypnosis, answer frequently asked questions, and provide practical solutions to help you stay on track. By the end, you'll feel equipped to handle setbacks with confidence and continue your journey toward mental mastery.

The Mindset for Success: No Failure, Only Feedback

Before diving into specific challenges, let's establish a guiding principle: there is no failure in self-hypnosis—only feedback. Each session, whether it feels productive or not, teaches you something about your mind, habits, and focus. Viewing challenges through this lens allows you to remain curious and resilient, turning obstacles into stepping stones.

How Self-Hypnosis Can Help You Overcome Challenges

The beauty of self-hypnosis is that it's not just a skill—it's also a tool to overcome the very challenges you face during practice. The techniques you're learning, such as relaxation, visualization, and affirmations, can be applied to address difficulties like inconsistency, doubt, or frustration. For instance:

- If you're struggling with wandering thoughts, you can use affirmations like "My focus improves with each session."

- If you feel stuck, you can visualize yourself breaking through mental blocks and feeling confident in your progress.

By turning self-hypnosis into both a skill and a solution, you'll create a powerful feedback loop that strengthens your practice.

1. "I Can't Focus During Sessions"

Why It Happens:

- Overstimulation from daily life or technology.

- Unrealistic expectations of perfect focus.

- Lack of familiarity with the practice.

Solutions:

- Start Small: Begin with short sessions (2–5 minutes) and gradually extend them.

- Use a Guide: Listen to recorded scripts or use an app to anchor your attention.

- Acknowledge Wandering Thoughts: Instead of fighting distractions, accept them and gently bring your focus back to your breath, visualization, or affirmations.

- Practice Mindfulness: Spend a minute focusing on your breath or a single sensation before starting your session.

2. "I Keep Getting Thoughts Pop Into My Head During My Sessions"

Why It Happens:

- Your brain is naturally active, and it's common for thoughts to arise, especially when you're trying to relax.

Solutions:

- View Thoughts as Clouds: Imagine each thought as a cloud drifting across the sky. Acknowledge it and let it pass without judgment.

- Create a Mental Parking Lot: Visualize a space where you "park" your thoughts for later. Reassure yourself that you can return to them after your session.

- Use a Focus Anchor: Concentrate on your breath, a word, or a simple affirmation to bring your attention back.

3. "I Can't Visualize"

Why It Happens:

- Visualization may feel challenging if you're not naturally a visual thinker or if you're trying too hard to create a vivid image.

Solutions:

- Engage Other Senses: Visualization isn't just about sight—imagine sounds, sensations, or even emotions. For example, instead of "seeing" yourself climb a hill, feel the rhythm of your pedalling and hear the wind in your ears.

- Use Verbal Cues: Describe the scene in your mind using words, such as "I feel the warmth of the sun on my face and the smooth cadence of my legs."

- Start Simple: Focus on small details, like the color of your bike or the feel of your handlebars and build from there.

4. "Nothing Is Changing"

Why It Happens:

- Change through self-hypnosis can be subtle and incremental, leading to frustration if you're expecting immediate results.

Solutions:

- Track Progress: Keep a journal to note small shifts, such as feeling more relaxed or focused during rides.

- Reframe Expectations: Understand that self-hypnosis builds cumulative benefits over time, much like physical training.

- Focus on the Process: Trust that consistent practice will lead to changes, even if they're not immediately noticeable.

5. "I Don't Feel Relaxed Enough"

Why It Happens:

- High stress levels or tension can make it hard to achieve a relaxed state.

Solutions:

- Progressive Relaxation: Tense and release each muscle group, starting with your toes and working upward.

- Breathing Exercises: Use deep, rhythmic breathing to calm your body and mind.

- Set the Scene: Eliminate distractions, dim the lights, and use calming music or white noise.

6. "I'm Not Sure I'm Doing It Right"

Why It Happens:

- Misconceptions about hypnosis (e.g., expecting a trance-like state).

- Comparing yourself to unrealistic portrayals in media.

Solutions:

- Educate Yourself: Hypnosis is a natural, focused state—not a mystical or otherworldly experience.

- Notice Subtle Shifts: Even small changes in focus, relaxation, or mindset indicate success.

- Redefine Success: Progress can be as simple as feeling slightly more calm or focused after a session.

7. "I Don't Have Time to Practice"

Why It Happens:

- Competing priorities or viewing self-hypnosis as a "nice-to-have" rather than essential.

Solutions:

- Schedule It: Dedicate specific times, such as post-ride recovery or pre-bedtime.

- Pair With Habits: Combine self-hypnosis with stretching, warming up, or cooldowns.

- Shorten Sessions: Even 2–3 minutes can make a difference.

8. "I Don't Feel Hypnotized Enough"

Why It Happens:

- Expecting hypnosis to feel dramatic or trance-like.

Solutions:

- Trust Subtlety: Hypnosis often feels like focused calmness rather than a deep "trance."

- Focus on Benefits: Notice how your sessions influence your rides, mindset, or recovery over time.

Conclusion: Embracing the Journey

Troubleshooting self-hypnosis is part of the process. Challenges are not roadblocks—they're opportunities to refine your approach and grow your skills. By addressing common obstacles with curiosity and patience, you'll develop a practice that's both effective and sustainable. Remember, every session—no matter how imperfect—brings you closer to mastering your mind and unlocking your cycling potential. Keep moving forward, one session at a time!

17 SEASONAL STRATEGIES

Cycling isn't just about the miles on the bike—it's about adapting to the ever-changing demands of the season. Each part of the year brings unique challenges and opportunities, whether you're focusing on building base fitness in winter, racing at your peak in summer, or reflecting and recovering during the off-season. Self-hypnosis is a powerful tool to help you navigate these transitions with purpose, resilience, and focus.

This chapter will explore how self-hypnosis can align your mental strategies with the goals and challenges of each season. By tailoring your visualizations, affirmations, and mental techniques to the time of year, you can maintain motivation, optimize performance, and sustain long-term growth as a cyclist.

The Cyclical Nature of the Cycling Year

Cycling, like life, flows through natural cycles of growth, intensity, rest, and reflection. Each season has its distinct rhythm:

1. **The Off-Season:** A time for rest, reflection, and laying the groundwork for the coming year.

2. **Base Training (Winter):** The foundation-building phase, emphasizing endurance, discipline, and consistency.

3. **Racing Season (Spring and Summer):** The period of peak performance, high stakes, and focused effort.

4. **Transition (Autumn):** A chance to wind down, recover, and assess your progress.

Each of these phases demands a different mindset. Self-hypnosis allows you to enter the right mental state for each season, ensuring that your mind is as prepared as your body.

The Role of Self-Hypnosis Across the Seasons

Self-hypnosis is uniquely versatile. Whether you're setting ambitious goals, recovering from intense efforts, or staying motivated in less exciting training periods, this tool adapts to your needs. Here's how self-hypnosis enhances each seasonal phase:

- Motivation: Reignite your passion when the weather or routine wears you down.

- **Recovery:** Accelerate physical and mental healing during periods of rest.

- **Focus:** Sharpen your attention when the stakes are high, such as during races or key training blocks.

- **Reflection:** Use hypnosis to evaluate past performances and visualize improvements.

With these principles in mind, let's dive into specific seasonal strategies, visualizations, and affirmations tailored to the unique demands of each time of year.

The Off-Season: Rest and Reflection

The off-season is a time to recharge, both physically and mentally. It's an opportunity to step back, reflect on your progress, and prepare your mind for the challenges ahead.

Visualization: Letting Go and Restoring Energy

1. **Relaxation Visualization:**

   - Close your eyes and imagine a calm, restorative space—perhaps a quiet forest or a serene beach.

- Visualize waves of healing light flowing through your body, repairing fatigued muscles and releasing mental tension.

- Repeat affirmations like, "With every breath, I restore my energy and prepare for growth."

2. **Reflection Visualization:**

- Picture yourself reviewing your cycling year as if watching a film. Focus on both successes and setbacks with curiosity rather than judgment.

- See each experience as a stepping stone toward future success.

Base Training (Winter): Laying the Foundation

Winter is all about consistency, discipline, and patience. It's the season where the hard work often feels thankless but is critical for future success.

Visualization: Building Strength and Endurance

1. **Endurance Visualization:**

- Imagine yourself on a long, steady ride through peaceful winter landscapes. Feel your legs working rhythmically, your breath controlled, and your heart steady.

- Repeat affirmations like, "Each ride builds my strength and endurance. I am becoming more consistent every day."

2. **Consistency and Discipline Visualization:**

- Picture yourself waking up on a cold, dark morning and putting on your kit with ease and determination.

- Visualize starting a training session and finishing it strong, proud of your discipline.

Racing Season (Spring and Summer): Performing at Your Peak

The racing season is where all your preparation comes to fruition. It's a time of high intensity, focus, and excitement.

Visualization: Race-Day Confidence

1. **Pre-Race Visualization:**

- Close your eyes and imagine the race start. Feel the anticipation, the buzz of the crowd, and the calm confidence in your body.

- Picture yourself executing your race plan flawlessly—taking the right line, pacing perfectly, and sprinting to the finish.

2. **Flow State Visualization:**

- Visualize yourself entering a state of flow during the race. Imagine every movement feeling effortless and precise.

- Repeat affirmations like, "With each pedal stroke, I am fully present and in control."

Visualization: Overcoming Challenges

1. **Mid-Race Struggles Visualization:**

- Picture yourself encountering a tough section—perhaps a headwind or a steep climb. Imagine reframing the discomfort as strength.

- Visualize overcoming the challenge with determination and repeat, "I thrive in difficult moments. I am becoming stronger with every effort."

Transition Season (Autumn): Recovery and Reflection

The transition season is a time to wind down, celebrate your accomplishments, and plan for the next phase of your cycling journey.

Visualization: Reflecting on Growth

1. **Celebration Visualization:**

• Picture yourself looking back on your achievements with pride. Focus on moments where you pushed beyond your limits and succeeded.

• Repeat affirmations like, "I am proud of my progress and excited for what's next."

2. **Goal-Setting Visualization:**

• Imagine writing your goals for the next season on a blank page. Visualize yourself achieving each one with clarity and determination.

Conclusion: Embracing the Seasons

Cycling is a year-round journey, and self-hypnosis helps you thrive in every phase. Whether you're resting in the off-season, building your base in winter, performing in summer, or reflecting in autumn, these tools ensure that your mind is aligned with your body's goals. By using the visualizations and affirmations tailored to each season, you'll unlock a new level of focus, resilience, and performance.

Each season presents its own challenges and opportunities, but with self-hypnosis, you're equipped to make the most of every moment. Let's keep riding toward growth, success, and balance—one season at a time.

18 Mental Tools for Group Rides and Team Dynamics

Cycling may feel like a solo sport when you're grinding out a time trial or riding solo, but the dynamics of group rides and team events introduce an entirely different set of mental and physical challenges. From managing the pressure to keep up with a group to fostering effective communication and trust within a team, the psychological demands of group cycling can be as intense as the physical ones. Whether it's a friendly weekend ride, a training session, or a competitive team race, the key to success lies in mastering the mental tools required to navigate group dynamics.

This chapter will explore the unique challenges of group cycling, strategies for improving collaboration, and the transformative power of self-hypnosis and visualization—both individually and as a team. We'll also emphasize how a trained sports hypnosis practitioner can elevate team performance through guided group hypnosis sessions, fostering cohesion and aligning everyone's focus on a shared goal.

The Mental Challenges of Riding in Groups: Pressure and Competition

The Pressure of Keeping Pace

One of the most common challenges in group cycling is the pressure to maintain the group's pace. Whether it's a relaxed social ride or an intense training session, the fear of falling behind can lead to anxiety, self-doubt, and overexertion.

Common Experiences:

- **Feeling outpaced:** Struggling to match stronger riders' speeds can erode confidence.

- **Overexertion:** Pushing beyond your limits to stay with the group can lead to burnout or loss of focus.

- **Fear of letting others down:** Riders often worry about slowing the group or being seen as weak.

Mental Strategies:

1. **Set personal goals:** Shift your focus from comparisons to individual progress, such as steady pacing or improving drafting skills.

2. **Practice reframing:** Replace negative thoughts like *I'm slowing everyone down* with empowering ones like *I'm building strength and learning with every ride.*

3. **Visualize success:** Picture yourself maintaining a steady cadence and confidently integrating into the group dynamic.

Navigating Competition in Group Rides

Even in non-competitive group rides, there's often an undercurrent of competition. While this can be motivating, it can also become mentally draining if you feel constantly measured against others.

Common Experiences:

- **Feeling intimidated:** Riding with more experienced cyclists can lead to feelings of inferiority.

- **Overthinking tactics:** Worrying about when to pull, conserve energy, or position yourself can detract from the ride's enjoyment.

- **Fear of judgment:** Concerns about being critiqued for your performance can amplify stress.

Mental Strategies:

1. **Focus on collaboration:** Treat group rides as learning opportunities rather than proving grounds.

2. **Stay present:** Shift your attention to your cadence, breathing, and surroundings rather than worrying about others' opinions.

3. **Celebrate small wins:** Acknowledge moments of improvement, like holding a strong position in the group or completing your pulls effectively.

Balancing Individual and Team Dynamics

Team settings, especially in competitive events, require you to prioritize collective goals over individual ambitions. This shift can be mentally challenging, especially when sacrifices are necessary for the team's success.

Common Experiences:

- **Ego vs. teamwork:** Balancing personal goals with team objectives.

- **Effective communication:** Misunderstandings or unclear strategies can create frustration.

- **Managing pressure:** Feeling responsible for the team's success can heighten stress.

Mental Strategies:

1. **Adopt a team mindset:** Recognize that contributing to the team's victory is as rewarding as individual success.

2. **Use affirmations:** Repeat statements like *Working together makes us stronger* or *I am a valuable part of this team.*

3. **Visualize team success:** By using group visualization team members will be able to carry out particular strategies, situations more successfully or how they respond during frequently experienced setbacks.

Group Hypnosis: Unlocking the Power of Shared Visualization

While self-hypnosis is a powerful tool for individual cyclists, group hypnosis and visualization elevate the team experience to new heights. A trained sports hypnosis practitioner can guide your team into a focused, unified mental state that aligns everyone's energy and intentions. These sessions can be particularly valuable before high-stakes events or during team-building exercises.

How Group Hypnosis Works

1.   Pre-Event Focus Sessions:

A sports hypnosis expert leads the team through a guided relaxation and visualization session, creating a collective sense of calm and focus. This might include deep breathing exercises, progressive muscle relaxation, and a shared mental rehearsal of the event.

2.   Shared Visualization:

The team envisions executing strategies seamlessly—whether it's a smooth paceline, perfect race tactics, or overcoming challenges together. This shared imagery fosters a sense of unity and confidence.

3.   Team Affirmations:

Guided affirmations like *We ride as one, strong and united* or *Together, we achieve our goals* reinforce collaboration and trust.

Benefits of Group Hypnosis:

- Builds trust and cohesion among teammates.

- Aligns everyone's focus on shared objectives.

- Reduces pre-race nerves and interpersonal tensions.

- Enhances collective resilience in challenging moments.

Practical Tools for Real-Life Scenarios

Pre-Ride Preparation

Visualization:

- Picture the group working in harmony, communicating effectively, and maintaining a steady rhythm.

- Imagine yourself contributing confidently, whether leading the paceline or drafting efficiently.

Affirmations:

- *I am calm, steady, and prepared for this ride.*

- *The group works as one, and I play an important role.*

Mid-Ride Stress Management

Quick Self-Hypnosis:

- Use an anchor, such as pressing your fingers together, to trigger calm and focus during stressful moments.

- Visualize yourself staying composed when the pace increases or a teammate needs support.

Affirmations:

- *I am steady and resilient, no matter the challenge.*

- *I thrive in group dynamics and adapt easily to any situation.*

Post-Ride Reflection

Group Hypnosis for Learning:

- After the ride, gather as a team for a short guided reflection session. Visualize key moments and reinforce positive behaviors, such as teamwork, resilience, or overcoming obstacles.

Affirmations:

- *Every ride strengthens our bond and sharpens our skills.*

- *We learn and grow together as a team.*

Conclusion: The Transformative Power of Group Mental Tools

Navigating group rides and team dynamics requires more than physical fitness—it demands mental agility, emotional resilience, and effective collaboration. Self-hypnosis and guided group hypnosis are powerful tools that enable individuals and teams to thrive in these settings. With the help of a trained sports hypnosis practitioner, teams can unlock their collective potential, creating an environment where trust, focus, and confidence flourish.

By embracing these mental tools, you'll not only enhance your own experience but also contribute to the success and harmony of your team. Together, you can tackle every challenge with confidence, connection, and a shared sense of purpose. Let's ride as one!

THE CYCLIST'S MIND

Conclusion: Your Journey Ahead

As we reach the end of this book, I hope you feel inspired, empowered, and equipped with tools to elevate your cycling—and your mindset—to new heights. Together, we've explored the transformative power of self-hypnosis, visualization, and mental training techniques, and how they can help you not only overcome challenges but thrive in every aspect of your cycling journey.

From building a strong hypnotic foundation to applying advanced techniques for managing pain, accessing flow, and enhancing recovery, this book has been designed to give you practical strategies that can be integrated seamlessly into your training, racing, and even everyday life.

You've learned how to tap into the power of your subconscious mind, reframe setbacks as opportunities, visualize success with clarity and emotion, and develop resilience to stay strong when the going gets tough. Whether you're chasing a personal best, preparing for a key event, or simply aiming to find more joy and focus on the bike, these tools are here for you, ready to be used whenever you need them.

But remember, just like cycling itself, mental training is a practice. The more you engage with these techniques, the more natural and effective they will become. Your journey doesn't end here—this is just the beginning of what you can achieve with consistency and curiosity.

Let's Stay Connected

If you have questions, want to share your experiences, or need further guidance, I'd love to hear from you. You can reach out to me through my website at www.hypnovelo.com. It's a space where I share additional resources, updates, and insights to support you on your mental training journey.

I also encourage you to leave a review of this book, either on my website or wherever you purchased it. Your feedback not only helps me but also guides others who might benefit from these techniques to discover this resource.

Keep Moving Forward

As you continue to explore the potential of your mind, remember that cycling is as much about the journey as it is about the destination. Every ride, every challenge, and every breakthrough is an opportunity to grow—not just as a cyclist but as a person.

Thank you for allowing me to be a part of your journey. I wish you strength for the climbs, courage for the sprints, and joy for every mile in between.

Let's keep riding toward greater possibilities.

– Jamie Borg

ABOUT THE AUTHOR

Jamie Borg is a qualified Clinical Hypnotherapist who specializes in Sports Hypnosis for cyclists. He set up Hypno Velo (www.hypnovelo.com) in 2020 and has helped cyclists of all abilities in a number of countries. Jamie provides services including 1:1 hypnosis and hypnosis training, visualization sessions and also group/team training services.

Jamie is based in the UK and lives with his wife and three children.